A LIVING SACRIFICE

David Curtis Wiggs

Acknowledgments:

It has been many years since the LORD first gave me this burning desire to accomplish this book for the edification and benefit of His people. As it says in 1Corinthians 2:4-7:

There are different kinds of gifts, but the same Spirit. There are different kinds of service, but the same Lord. There are different kinds of working, but the same God works all of them in all men. Now to each one the manifestation of the Spirit is given for the common good.

I have obeyed the LORD, and it is for the common good that I believe His Spirit has prompted me to embark upon this project. Not everything I've written in this book, is necessarily spiritual, meaning there are some of my own opinions here and there throughout the book, but the totality of the book, I have no doubt, was inspired by the Holy Spirit. I would first acknowledge Jesus Christ, the Author and Perfecter of my faith, for He alone is Worthy, and He alone is my First Love. It is His Spirit that fills me daily, moves me, and has His way in me. It is He who has inspired the very words within the pages of this book, and He who has gifted me for the Father's purpose, and for the glory of Jesus Christ.

I would next acknowledge my beautiful wife Tracy, you have taught me more about what it looks like from a practical perspective, of one who lives their daily life walking in the Spirit, then any one person I have ever known. The more God revealed Himself to me, the more I witnessed His very presence in you, in your daily brokenness, and in the overflow of the fruit of His Spirit, I love you Tracy. Next I want to acknowledge our 12 beautiful children, six of which are adopted, and one of which is our God child. Jonathan 25, Jacob 21, Joshua 21, Joel 17, Jeremiah 16, Jordan 14, Jared 12, Jonah 12, Jael 14, Jaden 11, Michayla 10, and Josiah 7.

God has used you all so very much, to touch my life, and has taught me so much more about His character, His grace, His mercy, and His love, through each one of you. God has blessed me beyond measure, having entrusted each one of you to me. To my children, I love you all so very much. God has used you all, in so many ways, to fill me with His wisdom, and to bring me to my knees; that He might fill me with His Spirit. I love you, and I am so very proud of you all.

Therefore, I urge you brothers, in view of God's mercy, to offer your bodies as living sacrifices, holy and pleasing to God-this is your spiritual act of worship. Do not conform any longer to the pattern of this world, but be transformed by the renewing of your mind. Then you will be able to test and approve what God's will is-His good, pleasing and perfect will.

Romans 12:1-2

Table of Contents:

Pages:

From the Author..*6-7*
Introduction..*8-9*

Chapter One: Therefore I Urge You
Brothers...*10-18*

Chapter Two: In View of God's
Mercy..*19-27*

Chapter Three: To Offer Your Bodies As Living
Sacrifices..*28-47*

Chapter Four: Holy and Pleasing to
God..*48-60*

Chapter Five: This Is Your Spiritual Act of
Worship..*61-72*

Chapter Six: Do Not Conform Any Longer to The
Pattern of This World.....................................*73-88*

Chapter Seven: But Be Transformed by The
Renewing of Your Mind.................................*89-107*

Chapter Eight: Then You Will Be Able to Test and
Approve What God's Will Is..........................*108-122*

Chapter Nine: His Good, Pleasing and Perfect Will
(The Sovereignty of God)..............................*123-137*

Chapter Ten: A Conclusion of The Matter...........*138-144*

From the Author:

I am not a renowned theologian, I do not have an English degree from an Ivy League College, and I certainly do not consider myself a writer. I am a Christian man who loves the Lord Jesus Christ with all my being, and a humble studier of His Word. One of my downfalls is my doubt, particularly about being a writer. Sometimes I think, maybe I'm not educated enough, or articulate enough, but it is at these moments of doubt, when my wife so graciously reminds me of what the Word of God says, particularly what the Sanhedrin said about the Apostles Peter and John in the book of Acts, and to which I cling:

When they saw the courage of Peter and John and realized that they were unschooled ordinary men, they were astonished and they took note that these men had been with Jesus.
(Acts 4:13)

This is who I humbly claim to be, an unschooled ordinary man, walking with Jesus. And it is in Christ, through His Spirit, I believe all of our talents and treasures are realized and appropriated for the glory of God and His Kingdom. I believe God has gifted me with the ability to put my thoughts down in writing, and I've always desired to be the author of a book, and thus this project has been on my heart for some time. I enjoy writing very much, and the Lord has used me many times to author letters to minister to believers and share the truth of the Good News with others. The desire to write this book became so strong that I believed it was the Lord compelling me. As I took hold of this desire and began meditating in prayer on whether it was the will of God or not, I began to take this project much more seriously. Of course with the desire to write, also comes the desire to read, and although I understand that man's wisdom is futile and God's Word of course is our ultimate authority and wisdom, I love to read devotionals and books on spiritual growth that are grounded in the Word of God.

Wisdom comes from God, but just as God raises up and empowers great speakers who proclaim His Word clearly and concisely, I believe He also raises up gifted writers who proclaim His Word in much the same way. Authors that I hold in high esteem, and truly enjoy are: C.S. Lewis, Josh McDowell, John McCarthur, Max Lucado, Lee Strobel, Jim Cymbala, Chuck Smith, and many others just to name a few. The insight I have received from these pastors and authors has helped me to grow in the knowledge of Christ, and has given me a deeper spiritual understanding of the Scriptures. *As iron sharpens iron, so one man sharpens another,* (Proverbs 27:17).

This of course, is my hope for this project. My hope is that God would use me, and His Spirit would flow through me; that my written word would sharpen my brothers and sisters in Christ. My prayer is that this book would encourage its readers to grow nearer to God, fall deeper in love with their Lord and Savior Jesus Christ, and help them to walk humbly with Him daily. It is God's Spirit that empowers each of us to accomplish His will, and we are all called to be His ambassadors, as we surrender everything to Him, that we might be used for His glory.

For we are God's workmanship, created in Christ Jesus to do good works, which God prepared in advance for us to do.
(Ephesians 2:10)

David Curtis Wiggs

Introduction:

This book is a leap of faith for me; however, it is important that I obey the Holy Spirit and not deny His quickening or the gift He has given to me. This project is no longer my own, I have given it completely to the Lord and I am compelled only by His Spirit and the strength and wisdom, He brings. Although this project will be challenging, I know that the Lord will guide and direct my steps through this process, and I will find it to be a wonderful and edifying experience, that will bring me nearer to God. I am completely trusting in the Lord and I am excited to see what He is going to accomplish through me. The truly challenging part for me, is that I remain focused on what the Lord wants to communicate through me. I have so many things on my heart that I want to say, but I must remain diligent and sensitive to the Spirit that I might chose my words carefully as I am led and inspired by Him and by Him alone.

As I begin, let me give you a little in-sight into the vision God has given me for this project. The Word of God tells us, that our lives are hidden with Christ in God, and in Colossians 1:26-27, it tells of this mystery that has been revealed, and this mystery, is "Christ In You." ***The mystery that has been kept hidden for ages and generations, but is now disclosed to the Lord's people. To them God has chosen to make known among the Gentiles the glorious riches of this mystery, which is Christ in you, the hope of glory.***

What I personally believe, is that this spiritual transformation and manifestation of Christ in us, is a truth many in the church do not fully believe, receive, or understand. We know that God is Spirit, and our relationship with God is spiritual, our transformation from the flesh to the spirit is spiritual, God's kingdom is spiritual, and we are called as believers to live spiritually, as we are filled with the Holy Spirit. Therefore, I believe it is necessary to approach the Word of God and our lives in Christ with a spiritual attitude.

.

This does not mean that we spiritualize the Scriptures as we imply spiritual application where there is none; however, at the same time it does not mean that we study the Scriptures simply from a practical human perspective, as we overlook deep spiritual truths, or worse, eliminate the spiritual all together. This is why the LORD has led me to Romans 12:1-2, where I believe, our spiritual lives in Christ, are summed up in these two very powerful verses.

Therefore, I urge you, brothers, in view of God's mercy, to offer your bodies as living sacrifices, holy and pleasing to God-this is your spiritual act of worship. Do not conform any longer to the pattern of this world, but be transformed by the renewing of your mind. Then you will be able to test and approve what God's will is-his good, pleasing and perfect will.

These two verses, I believe, are a literal call to action for every believer who would claim to have embraced Christ. I believe these verses are also a call to holy living and a complete road map leading every believer down the road of righteousness, which leads to true brokenness, which then leads to the filling of the Holy Spirit, and the ability for the believer to be governed by the Spirit in daily living. It is walking in the Spirit that empowers every believer to become more than conquerors, and live a victorious Christian life. And as you will see, living in obedience to these two verses, as the totality of Scripture is applied, we will find the answer to Christian living.

As we truly lay down our bodies as living sacrifices in true brokenness, abiding in Christ, we then learn in this condition that we can be filled with the Holy Spirit. As we learn to be surrendered to the power of God, everything else will fall in line with the will of God. And this is exactly what the end of verse two says: ***Then you will be able to test and approve what God's will is-His good, pleasing and perfect will.*** And so I implore you my friend, let us come and reason, and explore these verses, together.

CHAPTER ONE:

Therefore, I Urge You Brothers..............

I remember a pastor who would always say, "You have to ask yourselves, what's the therefore there for." And in this chapter I will discuss the *"therefore"* thoroughly, because what our response ought to be to everything that the Apostle Paul has written in the book of Romans, in chapters one through eleven, in my opinion, is summed up in the first two verses of chapter twelve. In chapters one through eleven, the book of Romans proclaims the elementary gospel, and very elegantly expounds upon salvation history. It is extremely descriptive on the subjects of the grace and mercy of God, our salvation, our justification and our sanctification. It clearly reveals to us our relationship to God before Christ, and our new life in Christ. The resounding themes include, that God is holy and man is sinful, God is our Judge and we are all under judgment, our sinfulness points us all toward our need for a Savior, and it is the Christ, the Son of God who has come to redeem us by grace through faith. Therefore, Paul is saying, in light of all that God has done, I urge you! Listen to me! Do what I say! Your spiritual lives in Christ will depend upon it!

A Living Sacrifice: Chapter One

Have you ever refused to heed the advice of someone? Why? Was it because the advice was not sound, or was it because you simply wanted things done your own way? We all want to do things our own way, and at times we might even seek out advice, but all the while having no sincere intention of doing things any other way then the way we have already planned. It's called pride! When under the influence of pride we can feel we have it all under control, and deeply manifested it erodes away at our very need for God. The Scriptures are full of advice, and it is the sin of pride that keeps us from heeding the full counsel of God. For we know that God's counsel is sound, so we can eliminate that excuse, and so then we are left to choice. We can ignore Paul's warning, *"therefore I urge you brothers,"* and refuse to give in to the urgency of his message, or we can turn from our sinful pride, and heed the counsel of our Lord! Pride is sin; in fact, aside from Satan himself, it is man's most dangerous enemy. We know that all sin separates us from God, and the sin of pride will quickly destroy our communion with God. Because we are continually tempted in our flesh, our fellowship with the Lord is always at risk of being hindered and the Holy Spirit quenched. Even though we might believe we are not in sin, and our conscience is clear before the Lord, we must always be broken before our God who is holy. Let us look at what James, the brother of Jesus, has to say in James 1:22-25, about simply listening to the authority of Scripture, yet not heeding its counsel, and thus not applying it to our lives.

Do not merely listen to the word, and so deceive yourselves. Do what it says. Anyone who listens to the word but does not do what it says is like a man who looks at his face in the mirror and after looking at himself, goes away and immediately forgets what he looks like. But the man who looks intently into the perfect law that gives freedom, and continues to do this, not forgetting what he has heard, but doing it---he will be blessed in what he does.

A Living Sacrifice: Chapter One

Therefore, the Lord urges us! Do not merely read, or study, or listen to the Word of God, but with the Holy Spirit's enabling, we are commanded to apply it to our every day life. Not just intellectually comprehending it, but doing what it says. Notice when we heed the counsel of God and do what it says, we will be blessed in what we do. This is what James is saying, and although James is speaking to us about obeying God's law, I believe it goes beyond that. I say this because I believe Christians tend to think that it is only the obvious commandments of God that we ought to heed and obey. Many overlook the fact that there are many verses that do not necessarily read as commands, but yet still a call to obedience. For a simple example, take Colossians 4:1a, ***devote yourselves to prayer***. Now we may pray daily, but do we truly devote ourselves to prayer? And if we don't necessarily devote ourselves to prayer, are we in sin? I believe we can be. It is because of our sinful nature that keeps us from fully drawing near to the Lord, but I also believe that through the power of the Holy Spirit we are able to conquer any hindrance that stands in our way.

This is exactly what I believe Paul is saying in Romans 8:8-14:

Those controlled by the sinful nature cannot please God. You, however, are controlled not by the sinful nature but by the Spirit, if the Spirit of God lives in you. And if anyone does not have the Spirit of Christ, he does not belong to Christ. But if Christ is in you, your body is dead because of sin, yet your spirit is alive because of righteousness. And if the Spirit of him who raised Jesus from the dead is living in you, he who raised Christ from the dead will also give life to your mortal bodies through his Spirit who lives in you. Therefore, brothers, we have an obligation-but it is not to the sinful nature, to live according to it. For if you live according to the sinful nature, you will die; but if by the Spirit you put to death the misdeeds of the body, you will live, because those who are led by the Spirit of God are sons of God.

A Living Sacrifice: Chapter One

    These verses give us great insight into the power of the Spirit of Christ that we have living in each one of us, who are in Christ. The same Spirit and power that raised Christ from the dead is the same Spirit and power indwelling you and I. But then we read that each one of us still have an obligation, and it is not to live according to the sinful nature. God is making it clear that even in Christ, we continue to have a choice. We can choose to still live according to the sinful nature, or we can choose to live according to the spirit. If we are to live by the Spirit, we must then choose to surrender everything in obedience to Christ, for this is how we will experience the freedom, and the victory, and the power that Christ's *sacrifice* and *resurrection*, has given to each one of us. The question and the challenge for every believer who truly is in Christ, is this, will we choose to truly surrender all, using now our freedom we have in Christ for righteousness, and thus taking hold of this victory we have already been given? All Scriptures that call us to action are commands from God. These Scriptures are there for our instruction and for us to obey, and it should be the priority and desire of every believer, to live according to all of the Lord's counsel, and instruction. We see this in 1Timothy 3:16-17: ***All Scripture is God-breathed and is useful for teaching, rebuking, correcting and training in righteousness, so that the man of God may be thoroughly equipped for every good work.***

    God's work is accomplished and equipped only by the power of the Holy Spirit through the instruction of His Word, and we receive His direction and guidance only by every Word that is God breathed, as all Scripture is from the mouth of God. Can we receive direction and guidance through other believers, and directly from the Lord outside of reading the Scriptures? Yes of course, but we can also receive direction and guidance that may not be from the Lord. So, ultimately where must we go to confirm that the counsel we have received is sound?

A Living Sacrifice: Chapter One

To God Himself, for all scripture is God breathed, therefore all that we do must line up with His Word. And living according to the Word of God is where in lies our victory. In James 4:8 it says this, **come near to God and he will come near to you.** If we know God, or rather if we are now known by God, through a relationship with His Son, then having received Christ we have come near to God and He has come near to us. However, our sanctification is an on going process and our relationship with God through His Spirit is an interactive relationship. Therefore, going back to my example in Colossians 4:1a, we can simply pray daily prayers or we can devote ourselves to praying in the Spirit on all occasion. Which one do you believe will bring you nearer to God? Then of course, this should cause us to examine our hearts, I mean, we must ask ourselves honestly, do we want to draw nearer to God? Do we really want God to be in control, or do we allow God to govern only in part, thus maintaining some control over our own lives. Let me tell you my friend, that Jesus calls us to surrender all, and although we all struggle and continue to sin, I am not talking about perfection, I'm talking about having our minds fixed on things above, and not on earthly things, having a mature spiritual attitude, that defines a life governed by the power of the Holy Spirit. What does Jesus say about holding on to our own lives? Let's look at Luke 9:23-26.

Then he said to them all: "If anyone would come after me, he must deny himself and take up his cross daily and follow me. For whoever wants to save his life will lose it, but whoever loses his life for me will save it. What good is it for a man to gain the whole world, and yet lose or forfeit his very self? If anyone is ashamed of me and my words, the Son of Man will be ashamed of him when he comes in his glory and in the glory of the Father and of the holy angels."

A Living Sacrifice: Chapter One

    It's very clear that we are called to surrender our lives completely to Christ. When we do this, with the Spirit's enabling, we will count the cost, and we will live our lives sold out for the glory of God. However, unless we have this daily attitude, acknowledging that we are commanded to obey and surrender our lives completely to Christ, this will never happen, and although salvation has come, we will live defeated Christian lives. What we put into action is what is in our hearts, and our attitudes, will always reflect our hearts. Unless we learn to surrender everything in obedience to Christ, this will only lead to our being ashamed of Him and His words, as we continue to live out our faith in the flesh. I realize we all have lives to live, jobs to attend to, children to raise up, (which are all God's calling), and living for Christ is not as black and white as I make it seem, but again, I'm not talking about spiritual perfection but having a spiritual attitude toward our relationship with Jesus, which I believe the Scriptures teach. Attitude is what will reflect our character and our character is what also reflects what is in our hearts. If Christ has given us a new heart, and we are a *new creation* in Christ, then there ought to be the evidence of such a transformation. I'm speaking spiritually, and not about simply having a good attitude, or moral convictions from a human perspective. We tend to allow our feelings to control our attitudes and judge one another on an emotional level. Now I would agree that what takes place in our lives spiritually, of course, definitely affects us outwardly, but I believe it is still possible, in the flesh, to have a great attitude in life as a Christian, and yet still lack communion with God, and thus remaining unchanged in our hearts. You may be asking yourself, at this point, how do we get this attitude I'm talking about?

A Living Sacrifice: Chapter One

We must immerse ourselves in the Word of God, and allow the Holy Spirit to transform our minds. Soon we will understand that God's ways are not our ways, and that to surrender our lives means to deny ourselves, rid ourselves of our own will, as we allow the Spirit to completely renew who we are; in other words, transform us in our mind, heart and soul. Remember, we are a *"new creation,"* in Christ, and we are not our own, but have been bought with His precious blood. Just as Christ freely laid down His life for us, we also must be willing to freely surrender all to Him. Now I believe that there are many in the church who remain unchanged in light of what Christ has done for them, and it is not necessarily because of unbelief, but rather a choice to remain in their un-surrendered lives. When we are unwilling to leave the world's influence behind, we will no doubt continue to walk according to the flesh, and not according to the spirit, and again, I believe this occurs not necessarily because they do not have the Holy Spirit, but because they refuse to surrender and be filled with Him, abiding fully in the Lord.

We know that **the fruit of the Spirit is love, joy, peace, patience, kindness, goodness, faithfulness, gentleness and self-control,** (Galatians 5:22-23a), and we tend to interpret these attributes and give them human significance; whereas, I believe these attributes are completely of God and are given to us by His Spirit and are spiritually manifested in us, in power, only as we make the choice to surrender our lives to Jesus Christ. Now, we know, of course, that even those in the world are able to display these attributes, but the difference being, though they do not know or acknowledge God, in their ignorance, through solely human effort, they display qualities that flow forth from their creature, which simply goes to prove, we have all been created in the image of God.

A Living Sacrifice: Chapter One

The Scriptures tell us, that God has revealed His invisible qualities, His eternal power and His divine nature to all creation, and that His Spirit convicts even those in the world of sin. However, as believers, having been born of the spirit, we must make the choice to either remain living according to our flesh, or choose now to live according to our spirit, as we surrender to the power of God, and as we seek to be filled with the Holy Spirit. As I close, much of what I have discussed in this chapter will definitely be reiterated, specifically in Chapter 7. Being transformed by the renewing of our minds is accomplished by the Spirit through the study of God's Word, and where I believe our spiritual victory is set in motion, as we heed the full counsel of God's Word. This is why I believe Paul makes such a boisterous claim, "I urge you brothers!" He wants us to get it. And so do I, I want us to get it too. I will leave this chapter with a final warning shown us in Hebrews 2:1-4:

We must pay more careful attention, therefore, to what we have heard so that we do not drift away. For if the message spoken by angels was binding, and every violation and disobedience received its just punishment, how shall we escape if we ignore such a great salvation? This salvation, which was first announced by the Lord, was confirmed to us by those who heard him. God also testified to it by signs, wonders and various miracles, and gifts of the Holy Spirit distributed according to his will.

The above verse tells us, *We must pay more careful attention, therefore, to what we have heard so that we do not drift away.* Notice the *"therefore"* is the same *"therefore"* Paul begins his exhortation with, "T*herefore, I urge you brothers!"* Now today, we need to pay more careful attention to not only what we have heard, but also to what we have read. We must remember how blessed a generation we are to have God's Word, in its entirety, right at our finger tips.

A Living sacrifice: Chapter One

Our salvation and our relationship with the Lord, does not end, but just begins when we hear the message of reconciliation, and respond to the grace of God. So I too, like Paul, *I urge you!* Do not allow yourselves to daily drift away, but in light of what Christ has done, take heed of the full counsel of God's Word, and by His Spirit, grow in the knowledge and wisdom of Christ.

CHAPTER TWO:

In View of God's Mercy........

What do you think about when you think of God's mercy? Truthfully, what is the first thing that enters into your mind? It ought to be the mercy God has shown you. It has been said, that grace gives to us what we do not deserve, and mercy saves us from what we do deserve. While we were yet still sinners Christ died for the ungodly, us, and yes, there is no condemnation for those who are in Christ Jesus, but in our new found freedom, let us not forget God's mercy. Where were we before we received Christ as our Lord and Savior? Every part of our being was corrupt, we were enemies of God, separated from Him, and we were dead in our transgressions. But remember, God in His sovereignty had a plan for each one of our lives. Every sinful act we've ever committed, and continue to commit, we do so against our Lord Jesus and our God, Who by grace, through faith, has given us new life, and through it all has continued to pour out His mercy. Although unable to fully understand God's sovereign plan, fearing the Lord is the beginning of wisdom.

A Living Sacrifice: Chapter Two

To understand His mercy we must see ourselves as the objects of God's wrath we once were, and understand that we are sinful beings.

Psalm 51:1-6, written under the influence of the Spirit, King David brings this all to the forefront:

Have mercy on me, O God, according to your unfailing love; according to your great compassion blot out my transgressions. Wash away all my iniquity and cleanse me from my sin. For I know my transgressions, and my sin is always before me. Against you, you only, have I sinned and done what is evil in your sight, so that you are proved right when you speak and justified when you judge. Surely I was sinful at birth, sinful from the time my mother conceived me. Surely you desire truth in the inner parts; you teach me wisdom in the inmost place.

Notice that King David, opens the Psalm pleading for God's mercy, as he then goes on to give synonyms for God's mercy: *unfailing love, great compassion, the blotting out of our transgressions, the washing away of our iniquity and the cleansing of our sin.* Notice also, that it's not just a one time cleansing, but David goes on to write: *For I know my transgressions and my sin is **always** before me.* When we acknowledge that our sin is always before us, and it is against the Lord and the Lord only that we sin, we are acknowledging that God is proved right. In other words, it is God that tells us that we are utterly sinful, and thus, when we acknowledge that we are, we are acknowledging His truth that He has already spoken.

However, when we deny our sinfulness and never learn to completely surrender, we make God out to be a liar. In 1John 1:8-10 God's Word says this: ***If we claim to be without sin, we deceive ourselves and the truth is not in us. If we confess our sins, he is faithful and just and will forgive us our sins and purify us from all unrighteousness. If we claim we have not sinned, we make him out to be a liar and his word has no place in our lives.***

A Living Sacrifice: Chapter Two

Clearly this passage is addressed to believers. Now some believers might think that acknowledging their sinfulness is only something we do at the time of our conversion, when we first come to Christ, but Psalm 51 and 1John 1:8-10, makes it clear that we must continually acknowledge our sinfulness and confess our sins to the Lord. It goes on to say that if we claim to have not sinned, as I have already mentioned, we make God out to be a liar, but it is the last part of the verse that really interests me. **His word has no place in our lives**! When we study the Word of God, with the help of the Spirit, our heart and mind is changed, and as the Word is then applied to our lives, we learn to walk in step with the Spirit, as we become more and more equipped for every good work. It is when we fail to make a place in our lives for God's Word, that although our position with God remains secure, we become idle, right where the enemy wants us. We can become spiritually weak, unable to bear fruit and accomplish the work that God has intended for us to accomplish. I will talk more about this later, but know that God wants us in His Word, not only that we would come to know Him better, but also that we would know what is required of us as believers. Returning to Psalm 51, we can see clearly that David is broken before the Lord. Let us then talk about brokenness, and what exactly does it mean to be broken before the Lord? I think that if we could fully understand the depth of God's love, or look upon our sinfulness, and truly see how our disobedience breaks the heart of God, brokenness would come more easily. But we must understand, it is possible to have a deeper understanding of our sinfulness which then leads to a contrite heart and a broken spirit. One function of God's Holy Spirit, is to break us, convicting us deeply of our sinfulness. I believe many of us understand our sin only on the surface, and comprehend it only from a human perspective. I know that we are human of course, but we must remember we have been born again spiritually.

A Living Sacrifice: Chapter Two

Again, we have been made alive in Christ, and we are a *new creation.* God's secret wisdom has been made known to us through the power of the Holy Spirit, which now indwells us. We need to understand, the battle between the flesh, (our sinful nature), and the spirit, (our soul now alive in Christ), did not begin until the moment we were born again of the spirit. In other words, when we were in our sins, we were dead to the spirit and could live only in obedience to the flesh, our sin nature. In Galatians chapter 5:16-25, we are given insight into this conflict between our spirit that has been made alive by the Holy Spirit, and the sinful nature, that can still have control over us, as we can allow our desires and passions to produce sin in our hearts. However, those that are in Christ, have had the sinful nature crucified with its passions and desires, and with the Spirit's power and enabling, we can overcome the flesh.

So I say, live by the Spirit, and you will not gratify the desires of the sinful nature. For the sinful nature desires what is contrary to the Spirit, and the Spirit what is contrary to the sinful nature. They are in conflict with each other, so that you do not do what you want. But if you are lead by the Spirit, you are not under law. The acts of the sinful nature are obvious: sexual immorality, impurity and debauchery; idolatry and witchcraft; hatred, discord, jealousy, fits of rage, selfish ambition, dissensions, factions and envy; drunkenness, orgies, and the like. I warn you as I did before, that those who live like this will not inherit the Kingdom of God. But the fruit of the Spirit is love, joy, peace, patience, kindness, goodness, faithfulness, gentleness and self-control. Against such things there is no law. Those who belong to Christ Jesus have crucified the sinful nature with its passions and desires. Since we live by the Spirit, let us keep in step with the Spirit.

A Living Sacrifice: Chapter Two

At our conversion the Holy Spirit was at work convicting us of sin, and upon receiving Jesus as our Lord and Savior our eyes were opened to the evil within us. The Holy Spirit came into our beings establishing residency, manifesting spiritual rebirth, as we were made alive in our spirit, and dead to our flesh. Through the Spirit, we begin to see our sinfulness in light of God's holiness, and for the very first time we become conscious of just how far short we fall, moving us to repentance. This of course is true, only if we have had a true conversion, and the Holy Spirit in fact indwells us. Having a contrite heart and a broken spirit requires a deliberate and ever conscious awareness of our sin and of God's mercy.

In Christ we are all under grace and our position with God has been reconciled; however, our condition is still being made holy. God is still sanctifying each one of us, and although we have been cleansed and forgiven of our sins, we continue to sin, and fall short. I can tell you from my own personal experience with sin that I have learned that brokenness is needed in our daily lives, regardless if we think we have a clear conscience before God or not. To be broken before the Lord, we must constantly acknowledge, as King David did, our sinfulness before a holy God, and recognize our need for Jesus and the Spirit's power every moment of every day.

When are we to be broken before the Lord? Always! Having a broken spirit and a contrite heart means, that we like David, must acknowledge that our sin is always before us, and we are continually in need of repentance. The flesh is still present, and we are still utterly corrupt in our sin nature, and thus to reckon the old man dead, we must be broken before the Lord, as we seek to be filled with His Spirit.

A Living Sacrifice: Chapter Two

Because we are a *new creation*, now having been born of the spirit, having been imparted with the righteousness of Christ, His Spirit now enables and empowers us to live a righteous life, and reckon the old man dead. When our lives are held up to the light of God's holiness, it makes it real difficult to point our fingers, or focus on others, as we are now redirected to focus on our own brokenness, as we seek to be filled with the Spirit. As we walk filled with the Spirit, suddenly the Christian neighbors down the street seeking a divorce because of an adulterous affair, becomes an opportunity to pray, rather than gossip, and the scandal at church over an individual's struggle with alcohol, drugs, or pornography, becomes an opportunity to reach out. When we are filled, and under the influence of the Spirit, we will find, we will unconditionally and involuntarily begin showing grace and love to those that we thought would be impossible for us to do so. It's not that the sins of others are not a shock to us, but in our own condition, we have no right to turn our backs on others, in hypocritical judgment, especially our brothers and sisters in Christ. We must learn not to condemn others in a way that seems to say, "Look at them, how could they possibly have done something like that, I thought they were Christians?"

In Luke 6:41-42 Jesus gives us this warning: ***"Why do you look at the speck of sawdust in your brother's eye and pay no attention to the plank in your own eye? How can you say to your brother, 'Brother, let me take the speck out of your eye,' when you yourself fail to see the plank in your own eye? You hypocrite, first take the plank out of your eye, and then you will see clearly to remove the speck from your brother's eye."***

Do we have understanding from God that we are to judge one another's sin, yes. I believe we are to confront sin in the church and in one another, but the one Jesus is speaking of in the above passage, is the one who ignores their own condition and heart, while being willing and ready to judge that of another.

A Living Sacrifice: Chapter Two

When we see ourselves as sinners, then we recognize that the sins of others flow from a sinful and deceitful heart, much like our own, actually, exactly like our own! Again let me say, I am not in any way condoning sin, but we must allow the Spirit to convict us of our own sinfulness, and thus leading to our own brokenness.

When we are truly broken, understanding who we are in our own sinful nature, we begin to recognize and confess our sins before the Lord daily, eventually bringing us nearer to the cross where our own understanding of God's grace and mercy becomes much more clear, and personal; furthermore, we begin to comprehend Christ's sacrifice at Calvary more profoundly, and once again, on a much more personal level. When I reflect deeply that it was for **me** Christ went to the cross and took upon Himself the condemnation and punishment for **my sin**, I become less likely to think of myself above reproach, in and of myself, thus making it difficult to condemn others. ***Remind the people to be subject to rulers and authorities, to be obedient, to be ready to do whatever is good, to slander no one, to be peaceable and considerate, and to show true humility toward all men. At one time we too were foolish, disobedient, deceived and enslaved by all kinds of passions and pleasures. We lived in malice and envy, being hated and hating one another. But when the kindness and love of God our Savior appeared, he saved us, not because of righteous things we had done, but because of his mercy. He saved us through the washing of rebirth and renewal by the Holy Spirit,*** (Titus 3:1-5)

As we reflect upon this chapter's title, *"In view of God's mercy,"* why does Paul once again preference the crux of the passage in Romans 12:1-2, with this second exhortation? I believe it is to remind us, that our lives in Christ and the salvation He brings is a free gift, and not something we have earned or could ever obtain through our own human effort.

A Living Sacrifice: Chapter Two

It is because of God's mercy, in His sovereignty, He has chosen to love and forgive us in spite of our disobedience, and therefore, we ought to respond to this mercy with great adoration and worship, surrendering now, our bodies as living sacrifices, to Christ, whom has given us new life. The following passage in Romans chapter 11, makes this clear, that God has had mercy on us all!

Just as you who were at one time disobedient to God have now received mercy as a result of their disobedience, so they too have now become disobedient in order that they too may receive mercy as a result of God's mercy to you. For God has bound all men over to disobedience so that he may have mercy on them all. Oh the depth of the riches of the wisdom and knowledge of God! How unsearchable his judgments, and his paths beyond tracing out! "Who has known the mind of the Lord? Or who has been his counselor?" "Who has ever given to God, that God should repay him?" For from him and through him and to him are all things. To him be the glory forever! Amen.
(Romans 11:30-36)

How do we understand such an inconceivable act of love? God has chosen to save us, in spite of us, to bring us back to Him. And we must understand that although we benefit from this great act of kindness that has led each one of us to repentance, that it was all done for one purpose, and one purpose only, to bring us back into fellowship with Him, for His purpose, for His Kingdom, and all for His glory. And for His purpose, is where it all begins, as we move into chapter 3, and look intently into Paul's exhortation and challenge to every believer, that we would offer our bodies as living sacrifices.

A Living Sacrifice: Chapter Two

    You see it was for God's glory that He reconciled us back to Himself through His own Son, Jesus Christ our Lord, and it is for His glory also, that we be sanctified and equipped for every good work, which God has predestined and purposed, for each of us to walk in. Just as in God's sovereignty, He chose to save us, so also in His sovereignty, He has chosen to use us. Every believer is called, commissioned, and has been predestined, to accomplish God's work here on earth. We are God's workmanship, and He has predestined you and I to bring to a dark, lost and dying world, in word and in deed, His message of grace, mercy, faith, hope and love, and so *"In View of God's Mercy,"* we must ask ourselves, how shall we now respond?

CHAPTER THREE:

To Offer Your Bodies As Living Sacrifices………

Would you be willing at this very moment to lay your life down for someone you love, or for your enemy for that matter, someone you don't even know how to love? Would you be willing to die for Jesus? Would you be willing to give up your child over to death for the sake of another? God did! And just as Jesus Christ was *obedient* even to death on a cross, so we are called to be imitators of God and follow Him, taking up our own *cross* daily. What do I mean when I say that Jesus was obedient? The following passage will give us a better understanding into His obedience.

Consequently, just as the result of one trespass was condemnation for all men, so also the result of one act of righteousness was justification that brings life for all men. For just as through the disobedience of the one man the many were made sinners, so also through the obedience of the one man the many will be made righteous.
(Romans 5:18-19)

A Living Sacrifice: Chapter Three

So, just as Adam's one act of disobedience to God has brought to all men condemnation and death; so Christ's one act of obedience to the Father, (His sinless life and ultimately His sacrifice on the cross), has brought justification and redemption to all men. And we see also in this passage that Jesus is referred to as "the man," and this is significant because we know that Jesus was fully human and fully God, many times referred to by pastors and teachers as the God-Man. In His taking on the appearance of a man, Jesus walked blameless and without sin, accomplishing all righteousness in obedience to His Father. We know that Jesus, although conceived by the power of the Holy Spirit, and was God incarnate, He came into our world a human baby. Throughout Scripture we see the evidence of Jesus displaying the attributes of God and human emotion. Not that Jesus was incapable of displaying great power in His Deity, but instead, walked in obedience to His Father, as He surrendered and walked in His humanness until the Father chose it necessary for His power to be displayed. In one of the most powerful accounts of Jesus displaying human emotion, knowing that He was being called to take upon Himself the punishment of God for the sins of the world, and that His death on the cross was eminent, Jesus, the Son, cries out to God the Father in the Garden of Gethsemane, on the Mount of Olives. We see Jesus in such anguish that He began to sweat what was like drops of blood.

And being in anguish, he prayed more earnestly, and his sweat was like drops of blood falling to the ground.
(Luke 22:44)

Now I do not know to be certain, if Luke is referring to thicker drops of sweat than normal, or if Luke is describing the fact that actual blood was mixed in with His sweat. However, we must remember that Luke was a doctor, and would have been the one to pay careful attention to the details of Jesus' condition.

A Living Sacrifice: Chapter Three

We do know however, of a true human condition called *Hematidrosis* which can occur while under intense mental suffering as a person might experience the capillary veins in the sweat glands of the skin, to breakdown, rupture, and cause bleeding. But regardless of what Luke was describing, we do know that Jesus was in grave mental agony.

Jesus went out as usual to the Mount of Olives, and his disciples followed him. On reaching the place, he said to them, "Pray that you will not fall into temptation." He withdrew about a stone's throw beyond them, knelt down and prayed, "Father, if you are willing, take this cup from me; yet not my will, but yours be done." An angel from heaven appeared to him and strengthened him. And being in anguish, he prayed more earnestly, and his sweat was like drops of blood falling to the ground.
(Luke 22:39-44)

Put yourself in your Savior's sandals, if you knew that you were going to die, not because you were sick and feeble, but because you were going to be subjected to human torture and were going to suffer excruciating pain, until your body was given over to death, do you think you would cry out to God to take it from you? We see that this is exactly what Jesus was doing. In His humanity, He was in anguish knowing that His gruesome and agonizing death was eminent, and then, we have to wonder as well, if Jesus knew that by taking upon Himself the Father's wrath for the sins of the world, that He would have to be temporarily separated from His communion with His Father in the process. But although Jesus was in anguish, He was obedient to the Father's will. He cried out to the Father, that if the Father was willing to take the cup of His wrath from Him, to do so, but notice Jesus says, ***"Not my will, but yours be done."***

A Living Sacrifice: Chapter Three

Jesus was obedient to the Father's will, He knew that He was sent to do the will of His Father, and that soon He would accomplish one last final act of obedience, in which He would freely lay down His life at Calvary. And I am so joyous that Jesus was obedient, even to death on a cross! We see that Jesus was not only obedient, but it actually brought Him joy to know of the glory His sacrifice would bring to God the Father and His Kingdom. That His sacrifice would redeem us all, and would bring us back into sweet fellowship with our Creator.

Let us fix our eyes on Jesus, the author and perfecter of our faith, who for the joy set before him endured the cross, scorning its shame, and sat down at the right hand of the throne of God.
(Hebrews 12:2)

When we look at Christ's suffering and His cross we must view it in two different ways. Although unpleasant, we need to see the cross as an ugly instrument of death, and reflect on the graphic images left to the imagination of the excruciating suffering of one being beaten and flogged, and ultimately nailed to the cross, thus realizing because of our sin, the length in which Christ went to redeem us.

But also we must reflect on the cross as a beautiful instrument of God's love. For in all of Christ's suffering and in His shed blood, as I take from an unknown author who once said, *"it was not the nails in His hands or the nail in His feet, but His love for you and I that held Him to the cross."* Just as the Scriptures tell us, that without the shedding of blood there is no forgiveness of sin, and also that Christ, the author of our salvation, was made perfect through suffering, we see God's sovereign will being accomplished through the cross.

This making it clear, that there was no other way but for Jesus, the Son of God, to suffer His Father's wrath, taking upon Himself the punishment for our sins, *a living sacrifice*, if you will.

A Living Sacrifice: Chapter Three

But we see Jesus, who was made a little lower than the angels, now crowned with glory and honor because he suffered death, so that by the grace of God he might taste death for everyone. In bringing many sons to glory, it was fitting that God, for whom and through whom everything exists, should make the author of their salvation perfect through suffering.
(Hebrews 2:9-10)

Now that we have reflected on the obedience of Christ, what do the Scriptures say about our responsibility to this call to obedience, and what does it truly mean to offer our bodies as living sacrifices? If our heavenly Father required obedience from His Only begotten Son, how much more do you think He requires it of us? We are commanded to follow Jesus in every way, and Jesus Himself gives us this exhortation:

Then he called the crowd to him along with his disciples and said, "If anyone would come after me, he must deny himself and take up his cross and follow me. For whoever wants to save his life will lose it, but whoever loses his life for me and for the gospel will save it.
(Mark 8:34-35)

Again, Jesus Himself calls us to deny ourselves and take up our cross. To deny ourselves is not as simple to accomplish as it sounds; however, Jesus is telling us that we are to surrender our own will to do the will of God. Jesus is calling us to follow Him, and that to follow Him means to abide in Him, as we trust only in His ways, and in His will for our lives.

A Living Sacrifice: Chapter Three

    Furthermore, we also see here Jesus using the cross, an ugly instrument of death, not only as a prediction of the excruciating death He would die, but also a metaphor to show us that in denying ourselves we must count the cost in order to follow Him, that in following Christ, no matter what circumstance we might find ourselves in, we will continue to abide, obey and worship Jesus as Lord of our lives. Not only are we called to obedience and to deny our own will, but just as Christ suffered, we too are called to suffer for His name sake. 1Peter 2:21 says this: ***To this you were called, because Christ suffered for you, leaving you an example that you should follow in his step.*** Now this does not mean that God requires all to suffer an excruciating death, but in light of Christ's suffering we are called to be steadfast in the faith, in the face of persecution, trials and tribulations, that are sure to come when we are surrendered to the LORD and living devoted to the gospel. Furthermore lest we forget, many throughout history have given their lives for the sake of the gospel of Jesus Christ. And as the Apostle Peter, inspired by the Spirit, writes of suffering, we can look to the historical record and see that Peter himself was crucified upside down at his request, not wanting to die in the same manner as our LORD.

> ***Therefore, since Christ suffered in his body, arm yourselves also with the same attitude, because he who has suffered in his body is done with sin. As a result, he does not live the rest of his earthly life for evil human desires, but rather for the will of God.***
> (1Peter 4:1-2)

    In Philippians chapter 2, the Scriptures give us even greater insight into the responsibility of every believer to diligently follow Jesus. It goes even further to say, that not only are we called to be obedient, but we are called to actually take on the attributes of Christ, and imitate His example.

A Living Sacrifice: Chapter Three

If you have any encouragement from being united with Christ, if any comfort from his love, if any fellowship with the Spirit, if any tenderness and compassion, then make my joy complete by being like- minded, having the same love, being one in spirit and purpose. Do nothing out of selfish ambition or vain conceit, but in humility consider others better than yourselves. Each of you should look not only to your own interests, but also to the interests of others. Your attitude should be the same as that of Christ Jesus: Who, being in very nature God, did not consider equality with God something to be grasped, but made himself nothing, taking the very nature of a servant, being made in human likeness. And being found in appearance as a man, he humbled himself and became obedient to death- even death on a cross! Therefore God exalted him to the highest place and gave him the name that is above every name, that at the name of Jesus every knee should bow, in heaven and on earth and under the earth, and every tongue confess that Jesus Christ is Lord, to the glory of God the Father.
(Philippians 2:1-11).

Every verse in the above passage is breathtaking, and I would encourage you to read the passage more than once; in fact, I would encourage you to meditate on the whole chapter. In context however, I would point your attention to the verses that exhort and call us to be like-minded and having the same attitude of Christ. Do we really think that as believers in Christ that we are any less obligated or should be any less devoted to living a life obedient to the will of God, than Christ Himself? What I mean by this is, if Jesus Christ, the God and Creator of heaven and earth, humbled Himself, came down from His Heavenly Throne, in human likeness made Himself nothing, taking on the very nature of a servant, if God did this, then what makes you and I think we are required to do anything less.

A Living Sacrifice: Chapter Three

We are called to be servants, and our Lord and Savior Jesus Christ was the greatest servant of them all. Through His example, Jesus has given us everything we need to follow and walk in His footsteps, and has not left us or forsaken us, but has given us the power to do so, the question is, will we follow?

So then, what does being a servant and sacrifice look like to the believer? We have already discussed the sacrifice of Christ that has brought us into a right relationship with God, through the washing and cleansing of our sin. In terms of humbling ourselves in the offering of our earthly vessels, we know that we are not required physically, to give up our lives unto death under most circumstances, but surrender them spiritually to God as an act of worship, but what does it mean to sacrifice and what is it that we sacrifice? When we are walking in the flesh, true sacrifice becomes non-existent in our busy lives; however, without sacrifice, it is our spiritual growth that becomes non-existent, and as the Spirit is then hindered and even quenched, so too is our communion with God.

To give a practical example, we see those in the world, having convictions and making sacrifices, even unbelieving parents love their children and understand their need to make sacrifices for them. But for those of us in Christ, we need to understand, that our love and sacrifice comes from the Lord. We must understand our children are not our own, but have been entrusted to us, and are a blessing from God. Our ability to unconditionally love them, and make sacrifices for them, comes form the Lord. The distinction I am trying to make is that when we are spiritually minded, we begin to understand our faith is centered in sacrifice, as we are commanded to lay down our lives and live a life of sacrifice, but as believers, we must understand true sacrifice is only accomplished in our selfless attitude toward God, trusting Him in all areas of our lives, as we abide in Him, and walk in step with His Spirt.

A Living Sacrifice: Chapter Three

Sacrifice is the work of the Spirit, and the one surrendered to the Spirit, will be the one to serve God sacrificially. We must choose today whom we will serve, and the Scriptures tell us, we can only serve one master. Where there is a surrendering and true sacrifice unto the Lord, there is a dying to self, but where there is loyalty to the world, there is every kind of idolatry. There are many acts of worship that can be considered sacrifice in the Scriptures. In order to give complete but yet brief examples, I will use three acts of sacrifice that the Lord commands and that are pleasing to Him. The three acts of sacrificial worship that best apply in our self indulgent lives in the world we live in today, are *fasting*, *fleeing sexual immorality,* and *fleeing the love of money.*

The Lord requires daily surrender, and we are called to lay down our bodies as living sacrifices, which means, to completely surrender our wills to Him. In order to illustrate the passion and deep submission required in serving the Lord, though in no way exhaustive, I will expound using practical life application, in order to simply show how sacrifice is required if we are to serve Christ, and leave the things of this world behind.

As I begin with *fasting*, what I would ask any believer regardless of their spiritual maturity, is are you aware that we are called to fast, and do you understand the significance of fasting in relation to the Spirit of God, your spiritual growth, and your relationship with God? I will take a moment to mention food in relation to fasting, simply to illustrate how we can abuse the provision of God, and how we can be obsessed and over indulgent. Many of us might be unwilling to admit it, but the fact is, people are obsessed with food. God's word warns us of the sin of making our stomachs our god; therefore, such sin is very possible.

A Living Sacrifice: Chapter Three

I only mention this, because when we are so obsessed with feeding ourselves, how difficult do you think it becomes for us to sacrifice a day, or even a few hours of fasting unto the Lord. We will make sacrifices and worship God with all our heart, mind, soul and strength, when we are surrendered and have no other gods before us. It cannot be accomplished through human effort, but occurs only as we are moved by the Spirit of God. This not only affects practically our service toward others, which becomes the evidence of true spiritual growth, but has everything to do with our spiritual attitude toward God.

What do the Scriptures say about fasting? In Isaiah 58:6-7 it says the following:

"Is not this the kind of fasting I have chosen; to lose the chains of injustice and untie the cords of the yoke, to set the oppressed free and break every yoke? Is it not to share your food with the hungry and to provide the poor wanderer with shelter-when you see the naked, to clothe him, and not to turn away from your own flesh and blood?"

In the above passage we see the Lord acknowledging His call for each of us to fast, but that fasting should not be done in vain, and that our acts of worship should be evidenced in our personal spiritual growth. Fasting is a form of worship which requires submission that denies our own bodies. In this condition, we grow nearer to the Lord, which by His Spirit then brings forth spiritual growth, as the chains that bind us are further broken and our freedom in Christ becomes more evident in our lives. As we grow nearer to the Lord there must also be the evidence of our spiritual growth, as our service and compassion toward others, becomes a way of life.

A Living Sacrifice: Chapter Three

In other words, fasting is more than simply what we do not eat, but an act of sacrifice and worship unto the Lord, that leads to spiritual maturity, which by the Spirit Himself filling us, reflects a spiritual attitude, which then produces good works. Reading further on in Isaiah we see again, that our fellowship with the Lord and our spiritual maturity, then becomes our reward through simply one act of obedience.

> *"Then your light will break forth like the dawn, and your healing will quickly appear; then your righteousness will go before you, and the glory of the Lord will be your rear guard. Then you will call, and the Lord will answer; you will cry for help, and he will say: Here I am. "If you do away with the yoke of oppression, with the pointing finger and malicious talk, and if you spend yourselves in behalf of the hungry and satisfy the needs of the oppressed, then your light will rise in the darkness, and your night will become like the noonday."*
> (Isaiah 58:8-10)

Let us now look at what Jesus says about fasting.

> *When you fast, do not look somber as the hypocrites do, for they disfigure their faces to show men they are fasting. I tell you the truth, they have received their reward in full. But when you fast, put oil on your head and wash your face, so that it will not be obvious to men that you are fasting, but only to your Father, who is unseen; and your Father, who sees what is done in secret, will reward you.*
> (Matthew 6:16-18)

A Living Sacrifice: Chapter Three

    In this passage, Jesus does not say if you fast, but when you fast. Jesus is commanding you and me to fast, but also Jesus goes on to warn us not to fast with wrong motives. Fasting must be done with a contrite heart and broken spirit, an act of true worship and sacrifice. So, from a practical perspective, sacrifice in regards to fasting, is the denying of self, by denying the body of food for a certain period of time. But what should our motive be when we fast? The Scriptures teach that fasting and prayer go hand in hand. Fasting becomes a spiritual act in which our bodies become spiritually in submission to God's Spirit. As we fast we become focused on the reason and purpose for our act of submission, and that is to draw nearer to God.

    When this occurs, as we draw nearer to God, God will draw nearer to us. As we pray in this condition we become more focused and are able to speak to God in a more clear and concise manner. In return, in this condition as we become more sensitive to the Spirit, we will be enabled by the Spirit to hear from God in much the same way. Again, when we are in submission to God's Spirit, we will hear much more clearly the Holy Spirit speak to us. As the passage in Matthew 6:19-18 suggests, fasting is a very private and personal act of sacrifice unto the Lord. If we are fasting or doing any act of worship to be seen by others, that they might see us as more spiritual, or we catch ourselves boasting about how spiritual we are, I would suggest that our motives are wrong and our hearts are in need of examining.

"Be careful not to do your 'acts of righteousness' before men, to be seen by them. If you do, you will have no reward from your Father in heaven.
(Matthew 6:1)

A Living Sacrifice: Chapter Three

When our acts of worship occur because of an out pouring of God's Spirit living in us, our acts of sacrifice and service will seemingly be effortless. Worshiping God, *in spirit and in truth,* is only possible when we are in the center of the Lord's will, and therefore human effort and wrong motives will never be a part of true worship. Let us now move on to what I believe is one of the greatest acts of sacrifice, and one that the Lord warns us adamantly about. Surrendering our bodies completely, and fleeing from the pleasures of sexual immoral behavior. In 1Corinthians 6:18-20 we find this exhortation: ***Flee from sexual immorality. All other sins a person commits are outside the body, but whoever sins sexually, sins against their own body. Do you not know that your bodies are temples of the Holy Spirit, who is in you, whom you have received from God? You are not your own; you were bought at a price. Therefore honor God with your bodies.***

Now, for men, I believe that lust, fornication, and all sexual immoral behavior that leads to bondage is a far more difficult struggle than for women; however, we are all guilty of indulging. Of course those of us who are married are able to indulge in healthy sexual behavior as long as it is kept within the marriage bed; however, even in marriage, we are all sinful people, and can be tempted. Those that are single, indulge in what they are commanded not to indulge in, and those who are married do the same. If marriage was the answer to changing our sinful heart, in the area of sexual sin, then the divorce rate in this nation, especially within the body of Christ, would be extremely low. Adultery however, in its many forms, is probably the number one reason for divorce in this nation, even in the church; therefore, we should not be surprised that Jesus allows the sin of adultery, to be one of two reasons a man or woman may divorce. God knows the hearts of men, and He knew we too would be living within an adulterous generation.

A Living Sacrifice: Chapter Three

In one of the strongest warnings to each of us, commanding us to lay down our bodies as living sacrifices, as we flee from sexual sin, is found in 1Thessalonians 4:3-8:

It is God's will that you should be sanctified: that you should avoid sexual immorality; that each of you should learn to control his own body in a way that is holy and honorable, not in passionate lust like the heathen, who do not know God; and that in this matter no one should wrong his brother or take advantage of him. The Lord will punish men for all such sins, as we have already told you and warned you. For God did not call us to be impure, but to live a holy life. Therefore, he who rejects this instruction does not reject man but God, who gives you his Holy Spirit.

We must remember that the flesh is weak and the heart is deceitful, and we will be tempted by our own sinful desires in a world full of sexual immorality, and let us not down play the power of Satan as well. In 1 Peter 5:8-9, it says this:

Be self-controlled and alert. Your enemy the devil prowls around like a roaring lion looking for someone to devour. Resist him, standing firm in the faith, because you know that your brothers throughout the world are undergoing the same kind of sufferings...

Now we can never blame Satan for our own desires and choices that lead to sin, and we must always rely upon the Spirit of God to strengthen us to repent and turn from temptation. God cannot be tempted by evil, and He has given us His promises. To those who are His, He is faithful and will never allow you and I to be tempted beyond what we can bare. God will always give us a way out, however we must take heed. Without His strength, as we walk through temptation, we will succumb every time to our flesh, as the spirit is willing but the flesh is weak.

A Living Sacrifice: Chapter Three

There are many passages in Scripture warning against sexual immoral behavior, and though the Scriptures may have been written over two thousand years ago, when we see the immorality in our world, it is easy to explain why the Word of God is full of warnings against sexual immorality, and how then the Word is active and living and applicable to our lives today. The Bible teaches that our hearts are deceitful and desperately wicked in every way, and God warns us to rid ourselves of all immorality. When we fill our minds and hearts with moral filth, we feed the sinful nature, and smother the spirit, which only sets ourselves up for failure. We are tempted by our own evil desires that fill our hearts, and so the evil we allow into our hearts, through our minds, will eventually conceive sin.

Therefore, get rid of all moral filth and the evil that is so prevalent and humbly accept the word planted in you, which can save you.
(James 1:21)

Pornography has destroyed millions of marriages, and has corrupted the minds and hearts of millions of men and women in the church, which Satan, I can assure you has been relentless in his attacks, and has gloated over every victory. We must understand, we allow Satan these victories in our lives, and as we walk in the flesh, we will have no ability to fight against the desires and passions that rule in our hearts; however, we must remember that we are a *new creation* in Christ, and we now have the ability to walk according to the Spirit.

A Living Sacrifice: Chapter Three

Those who are in bondage to sexual sin, are most likely addicted to pornography, or most certainly have had some problem with pornography at one point in their lives. Because God has created man and woman sexual beings, we struggle in the flesh with lust. Sexual intimacy is very beautiful and very pleasurable, the way God intended it to be within marriage, but unfortunately because of our sin nature, we stray, and it becomes very difficult for us to remain pure, especially when our pursuit of sexual pleasure is a natural part of our being. The problem is when lust becomes sin, and in the flesh, we all stray from God's perfect plan. God created sexual pleasure within the boundaries of the marriage bed between one man and one woman, and because we are all tempted with the sin of lust, we need to be wearing the full armor of God daily, or we will fall. We need the self control that only the Holy Spirit can produce. Adultery is a very serious sin, and most men and women, are fooled into believing, that adultery is committed only by a physical sexual act; however, Jesus tells us, that the man who looks lustfully after a woman has committed adultery in his heart. ***"You have heard that it was said, 'You shall not commit adultery.' But I tell you that anyone who looks at a woman lustfully has already committed adultery with her in his heart."*** (Matthew 5:27-28)

Therefore, in light of what Jesus exhorts, viewing pornography in and of itself is lust at its worst. Most men and women unfortunately even Christians, as they walk in the flesh, fail to acknowledge this because, in their minds, pornography is simply fantasy and not real; therefore, not harmful or even sinful. However, finding sexual pleasure in any form, outside of the marriage bed, is sinful period! My point? All sexual behavior outside of the marriage bed, is immoral in the sight of God. So then, how do we guard ourselves from this sexual immorality and keep our way pure? Through the Word of God, and by the power of the His Spirit.

A Living Sacrifice: Chapter Three

Psalm 119:9-11 says this: ***How can a young man keep his ways pure? By living according to your word. I seek you with all my heart; do not let me stray from your commands. I have hidden your word in my heart that I might not sin against you.***

We must know God's Word, as we remain in the study of God's Word; however, we must seek to be filled with the Spirit's power and remember it is the Holy Spirit that imparts to us God's wisdom, and enables us to walk in obedience to His commandments. Though it is the Spirit that empowers us, we see throughout Scripture, that there are practical steps we can take to honor God as we live this life of sacrifice. Take for example Job. Job made a covenant with his eyes not to look lustfully at other women. We must sacrifice our bodies to the Lord and make a covenant to remain sexually pure in word and in deed. We need to recognize that we are bombarded with sexual immorality daily, and that our minds are subjected to sexual temptations everywhere we turn. We need to recognize that the problem is the heart, and know that we must deal with, and surrender the deeply rooted sin within our hearts. Surrendering all to the Lord requires that we examine every area of our lives, and especially in this area of sexual immorality, where sacrifice must become a way of life, to live holy and pleasing to God.

The third and final act of sacrifice, is the sacrificing of our finances, with the spiritual attitude that everything we have belongs to God. Having things and having money is not the problem, it is when the love of money and our lust and our covetousness to have it all, becomes our god, and we place our trust in this idol, as we deny the Living God.

A Living Sacrifice: Chapter Three

When we fail to recognize God's sovereignty, that everything belongs to Jesus, and when we fail to acknowledge that everything has been created by Him and for Him, the sin of idolatry can easily set in. It will always be creeping at our door, as we will find ourselves trusting less in God, and more in the things of the world.

Whoever loves money never has money enough; whoever loves wealth is never satisfied with his income. This too is meaningless. As goods increase, so do those who consume them. And what benefit are they to the owner except to feast his eyes on them?
(Ecclesiastes 5:10-11)

We live in a world today where we are tempted at every turn to covet and to go after material things. We tend to want it all, and because it's all available, we fall into this trap the world has set for us. We turn away from our trust in God to provide all that we need, when we strive and set our own goals. We work long hours, and go after our careers and promotions, as we focus our minds and our hearts, on status and wealth. We covet, and all the while thinking, this is what is going to make us happier people. But if we are relying on things and money to make us happy, then what happens when it doesn't make us happy? The reality is, the love of this world will only make us more miserable and oppressed, leaving us empty, with an insatiable lust for more, that will never satisfy. When we sacrifice our finances, and all we possess to the Lord, when we are trusting solely in God for our provision, as we acknowledge all that we have is from God and belongs to Him, God will change our heart and our attitude. Trusting in God and acknowledging everything belongs to Him, does not mean we cannot have things or that having money is sinful in itself; however, we must always be examining our hearts before the Lord, for God looks intently at the heart.

A Living Sacrifice: Chapter Three

Remember, the LORD blesses, that we might bless others as He uses us for His purpose. When our hearts are changed and we learn to sacrifice our finances and possessions to the Lord, we become satisfied and content. When our hearts and our attitudes are changed, sacrificing our finances and possessions becomes an unconditional act of worship unto the Lord. We learn to tithe and give back to the Lord, we learn to give to others who are in need, and most importantly we learn to seek God in every decision we make regarding our money and possessions, which rightfully belong to Him in the first place. The greatest example of a true faith and trust in God despite having lost everything is once again, found in the book of Job. Because Job understood God's sovereignty and trusted completely in God's faithfulness, he refused to be defeated by his circumstances. Job not only lost his wealth and possessions but also his health, and his ten children, and though tempted by his own wife to do so, Job never cursed God, but continued to praise, and worship Him. Would we be able to do the same if we were to lose everything, or would we turn away and curse God, blaming Him for our circumstances, as we crumbled under the pressure?

I suggest to you that Job was not any more special to God then you and I, and Job did not have a secret plan to cope with adversity. No, Job's ability to cope is not a secret at all. Job was righteous, and he loved the Lord God with all his heart, mind, soul and strength. Job was able to deal with all that he had lost, because he had already, in his heart, sacrificed everything to God. Having lost everything we read of Job's reaction:

At this, Job got up and tore his robe and shaved his head. Then he fell to the ground in worship and said: "Naked I came from my mother's womb, and naked I will depart. The LORD gave and the LORD has taken away; may the name of the LORD be praised." In all this, Job did not sin by charging God with wrongdoing.
(Job 1:20-22)

A Living Sacrifice: Chapter Three

As Job tears his robe and shaves his head, we see Job's brokenness and lamenting spirit over his circumstance, and rightly so, and next we see Job fall to the ground, as I picture a man, on his face, with his body sprawled out on the ground, in complete worship and submission to the Lord. Job then acknowledges God's sovereignty by exclaiming the Lord's right to take away what He had freely given, and finally, Job did not sin by blaming God for his circumstances. You and I will have the same heart and attitude as Job, when we learn to sacrifice all that we have to the Lord and acknowledge that we are simply called to be stewards of everything the Lord has given us.

Although I have ended this chapter with practical life application, as I've given examples, of how we might sacrifice our lives to the Lord, through specific acts of worship. *"To Offer Your Bodies as Living Sacrifices,"* requires one thing, and one thing only, submission. We must be willing to surrender to the Lord, and at all cost to deny our own wills and devote ourselves solely to doing the will of God. Sacrifice unto God, is submission, it is obedience, it is selflessness, and it is surrendering to His Spirit. Everything comes down to denying our own will, and relying upon His Spirit, to live a life holy and pleasing to God, and walk in His will. In the next chapter I will expound upon the holiness of God, and discuss how He has called us all to live holy lives, to be holy, as He is holy.

CHAPTER FOUR:

Holy and Pleasing to God......

Therefore, prepare your minds for action; be self-controlled; set your hope fully on the grace to be given you when Jesus Christ is revealed. As obedient children, do not conform to the evil desires you had when you lived in ignorance. But just as he who called you is holy, so be holy in all you do; for it is written: "Be holy, because I am holy." (1Peter 1:13-16)

We must first understand that we have no righteousness of our own, and being or becoming holy is not possible by human effort. Even the most diligent commitment and devotion to living a good life, can never be good enough to bring about righteousness; in fact, Isaiah 64:6, says this: *All of us have become like one who is unclean, and all our righteous acts are like filthy rags; we all shrivel up like a leaf, and like the wind our sins sweep us away.*

And in Romans 3:10-11, it tells us: *As it is written: "There is no one righteous, not even one; there is no one who understands; there is no one who seeks God.*

A Living Sacrifice: Chapter Four

Because we are sinful people and we all fall short of the glory of God, holiness can only be accomplished through sanctification, which means to be set apart for God's purpose and glory. It is only the righteousness of God that is imparted to you and I through a faith in Jesus Christ that makes us acceptable in God's sight, and it is only through the power of His Holy Spirit, by which we are being transformed into a holy people. In fact, the Scriptures tell us in Romans 8:29, that we are being conformed to the very likeness of Christ Himself: ***For those God foreknew he also predestined to be conformed to the likeness of his Son, that he might be the firstborn among many brothers.***

Now, we can see in the previous exhortation in 1Peter 1:16, God calls us to be holy, and this of course is directed to believers. You see, only the indwelling of the Spirit can change our hearts and our attitudes, and guide us toward the holiness of God. Only believers have the indwelling of His Spirit, which God has given to every believer as a deposit sealing our inheritance, and marking us as God's very own until we leave this earth, and our souls enter into eternity. In Nelson's Illustrated Bible Dictionary, holy is described as follows: *a moral and ethical wholeness or perfection; freedom from moral evil. Holiness is one of the essential elements of God's nature required of His people. Holiness may also be rendered "sanctification" or "godliness." The word holy denotes that which is "sanctified" or "set apart" for divine service.*

God is holy! This spiritual truth is one of the most important truths God's Word reveals to us in relation to the character of our Heavenly Father. It is in His holiness that reveals to us that God is not only a God of love, but also a God of wrath and an all consuming fire. Because God is holy, our sin is what keeps us from coming into the presence of our Creator.

A Living Sacrifice: Chapter Four

Outside of grace, we are all unclean and therefore it is impossible for God in His holy nature to accept us, and thus we are separated from Him and under His wrath. God's holiness in its very essence must punish and condemn sin. Because you and I have sinned and have offended a holy God we stand condemned, and in light of God's holiness we stand guilty, and with no defense. But although it is because of God's holiness that we must be punished and condemned for our sinfulness, it is the exact same attribute of God, that saves us and brings us into a right relationship with Him. For it is the righteousness or holiness from God, that comes through faith in Jesus Christ to all who believe. We are made righteous in God's sight through His holiness by the Spirit of Christ which indwells every believer.

God made him who had no sin to be sin for us, so that in him we might become the righteousness of God.
(2Corinthians 5:21)

But now a righteousness from God, apart from law, has been made known, to which the Law and the Prophets testify. This righteousness from God comes through faith in Jesus Christ to all who believe. There is no difference, for all have sinned and fall short of the glory of God, and are justified freely by his grace through the redemption that came by Christ Jesus. God presented him as a sacrifice of atonement, through faith in his blood. He did this to demonstrate his justice, because in his forbearance he had left the sins committed beforehand unpunished-he did it to demonstrate his justice at the present time, so as to be just and the one who justifies those who have faith in Jesus.
(Romans 3:21-26)

A Living Sacrifice: Chapter Four

In Nelson's Illustrated Bible Dictionary, the word righteousness is described as follows: *Holy and upright living, in accordance with God's standard. The word righteousness comes from a root word that means "straightness." It refers to a state that conforms to an authoritative standard. Righteousness is a moral concept. God's character is the definition and source of all righteousness, therefore, man's righteousness is defined in terms of God's. It goes on to say: The cross of Jesus is a public demonstration of God's righteousness. God accounts or transfers the righteousness of Christ to those who trust in Him.*

We do not become righteous because of our inherent goodness. God sees us as righteous because of our identification by faith in His Son. Having looked briefly into the holiness of God, what does it mean then to live a life holy and pleasing to God? In Ephesians 5:8-10, it tells us to find out what pleases the Lord, and in Ephesians 5:15-18, it tells us to understand what the Lord's will is, and then goes on to give us understanding into how this is accomplished in our lives.

> *For you were once darkness, but now you are light in the Lord. Live as children of light (for the fruit of the light consists in all goodness, righteousness and truth) and find out what pleases the Lord.*
> (Ephesians 5:8-10)

> *Be very careful, then, how you live-not as unwise but as wise, making the most of every opportunity, because the days are evil. Therefore do not be foolish, but understand what the Lord's will is. Do not get drunk on wine, which leads to debauchery. Instead, be filled with the Spirit.*
> (Ephesians 5:15-18)

A Living Sacrifice: Chapter Four

Ephesians 5:15-18, ends with this exhortation, ***"Instead be filled with the Spirit!"*** And this is exactly how our knowledge and understanding of both, finding out what pleases the Lord, and understanding what the Lord's will is, are revealed, and what I believe the Scriptures teach, is the source of all spiritual life. For just as the Lord spoke through the Apostle Paul, ***"I have been crucified with Christ, I no longer live but Christ lives in me."*** It is Christ living in us that changes us, and so the Lord commands us, ***"Instead Be filled with the Spirit!"***

Going back to Ephesians 5:8-10, on page 51, we see it is through Christ that we have been changed. We were once in darkness; in other words, before receiving salvation through Christ, we were living in darkness living only to please the sinful nature under the influence of our own evil desires, Satan and the world; however, in Christ, having received His Spirit, we have now become light in the Lord. In the book of John verse 8:12, Jesus said, ***"I am the light of the world. Whoever follows me will never walk in darkness, but will have the light of life."***

Again in Ephesians 5:8-10, we are exhorted to live as children of light and that the fruit of the light consists of all goodness, righteousness and truth. It goes on to say, and find out what pleases the Lord. Well, we know that the light is Jesus, and therefore it is His very presence filling our inner being through His Spirit that brings us to the knowledge of what pleases Him through His Word, and gives us the power to walk in obedience to even the simplest commands of Scripture. Ephesians 5:15-18, goes on to exhort us, that we are not to live as fools, but understand what the Lord's will is. This brings us to the very essence of our relationship with God. Beyond our knowledge and hope of eternal life, we have been given understanding of why we have been born again and left here in the world, and it is for God's purpose, and for His glory that God might accomplish His will in and through us.

A Living Sacrifice: Chapter Four

Living a holy life as we are exhorted to do in 1Peter 1:16, and understanding what the Lord's will is, is accomplished only by being obedient to the final exhortation we find in Ephesians 5:18, **"instead, be filled with the Spirit."** We need to know that although God calls us to be holy as He is holy, it is not by our own effort. Although we read these exhortations over and over again throughout Scripture, we tend to look at them, and interpret them, from a human perspective, as if to think somehow it requires our own effort, ingenuity, or strength to live in obedience to them; however, although our obedience does require choice and thus free will, it is only through the power of the Holy Spirit that we can live in obedience to God's moral will. To try to be holy by our own human effort is futile, and I believe to be sinful. When we walk in the flesh, in our own effort, we are not trusting in God, His Spirit, and thus denying His power.

Let us now look at the exhortation just before, **"Instead, be filled with the Spirit."** It says that we are *not to get drunk on wine, which leads to debauchery.* What happens when we are intoxicated? Does not a change in our physical bodies occur? Of course we do not become void of our free will, but the intoxication does skew our rational and normal thinking and behavior. You might say that, we are under the influence, and as a Christian I find this analogy very interesting, because we can choose to be under the influence of our sinful nature, or we can choose to yield to God and be under the influence of His Spirit.

To be filled with the Spirit, means to be under the influence and the control of the Spirit. And If God commands us to be filled with His Spirit, then it must mean that it is possible to not be filled, and thus empty of the Spirit's power.

A Living Sacrifice: Chapter Four

JESUS PROMISES THE HOLY SPIRIT!

But I tell you the truth: It is for your good that I am going away. Unless I go away, the Counselor will not come to you; but if I go, I will send him to you. When he comes, he will convict the world of guilt in regard to sin and righteousness and judgment: in regard to sin, because men do not believe in me; in regard to righteousness, because I am going to the Father, where you can see me no longer; and in regard to judgment, because the prince of this world now stands condemned. "I have much more to say to you, more than you can now bear. But when he, the Spirit of truth, comes, he will guide you into all truth. He will not speak on his own; he will speak only what he hears, and he will tell you what is yet to come. He will bring glory to me by taking from what is mine and making it known to you. All that belongs to the Father is mine. That is why I said the Spirit will take from what is mine and make it known to you.
(John 16:7-15)

Jesus tells His disciples, that soon He would be gone, but that He would not leave them alone or without help. The Holy Spirit which Jesus refers to as the Counselor, or One who comes along side to help and to guide and direct, would soon be given to them. In John 20:22, Jesus breaths on His disciples and says, "Receive the Holy Spirit." ***And with that he breathed on them and said, "Receive the Holy Spirit."***

This parallels the Father breathing life into Adam, in the first creation, with Jesus breathing on His disciples, in the rebirth, as they now become, a *"new creation,"* (2Corinthians 5:17).

A Living Sacrifice: Chapter Four

I believe that the Holy Spirit was given to the disciples at that moment we see in John 20:22, when Jesus breathed on them, and that the Day of Pentecost in Acts 2, when the disciples and the other believers received the power of the Holy Spirit, that these were two different events all together. I believe the receiving of the Holy Spirit at conversion is different from the Holy Spirit coming upon us, or known as, the baptism of the Spirit. This is when I believe we are filled with God's dynamic power, which then empowers every believer to accomplish His purpose, and live in accordance with His moral and sovereign will. In Acts 1:4-8, we read the account of Jesus telling His disciples of the Father's gift, the promised Holy Spirit. Jesus goes on to tell them, that they would be baptized with the Holy Spirit, and we know this is after the disciples had received the Holy Spirit, in John 20:22. In this account in Acts, Jesus is much more specific about the power that they will receive when the Holy Spirit comes upon them. On one occasion, while Jesus was eating with them, he gave them this command: ***"Do not leave Jerusalem, but wait for the gift my Father promised, which you have heard me speak about. For John baptized with water, but in a few days you will be baptized with the Holy Spirit." So when they met together, they asked him, "Lord, are you at this time going to restore the kingdom to Israel?" He said to them: "It is not for you to know the times or dates the Father has set by his own authority. But you will receive power when the Holy Spirit comes on you; and you will be my witnesses in Jerusalem, and in all Judea and Samaria, and to the ends of the earth."*** (Acts 1:4-8)

The Scriptures clearly tell us, that the Holy Spirit in us, is different than the Holy Spirit coming upon us. One, is receiving the Holy Spirit which occurs in every believer's life at conversion, and the second is the baptism, or the gift of the Holy Spirit, which occurs in a believer's life when we are abiding in the Lordship of Jesus Christ, surrendered to God, and seeking to be filled with His Spirit.

A Living Sacrifice: Chapter Four

Those in Christ, we all have the Holy Spirit, and His power is unchanging, but the question is not how much of the Holy Spirit does a believer have, but how much of the believer's life is in submission and surrendered to the Spirit, trusting and not doubting in His power. Notice Jesus' command to the disciples in Acts 1:4: *Jesus tells them to remain in Jerusalem and wait for the gift the Father promised, the Holy Spirit.* This is very interesting to me, because it must have taken great resolve for the disciples of Jesus to remain in the very town where their Lord was just crucified, knowing that as followers of Jesus they would be recognized, and for fear that they too, would be persecuted, or even brought to death.

But I believe they were already being guided and given strength by the Spirit within them, and maybe, just maybe, they were trusting in Jesus' words and were left with the understanding that something was going to happen, and that something would be very powerful. And we see in Acts 1 the disciples returning to the town of Jerusalem from the Mount of Olives. They gathered together to pray constantly and wait on the Lord, Acts 1:14. **They all joined together constantly in prayer, along with the women and Mary the mother of Jesus, and with his brothers.**

We see in the Scriptures, that after our Lord's resurrection, when Jesus appeared to His disciples, that yes they were amazed and astonished and over taken with great joy and elation, and it is after His resurrection when Jesus breathed upon His disciples when they first received the Holy Spirit, but this is not the moment in Scripture, we see them going out and being witnesses for the gospel of Jesus Christ. In fact, in the gospel of John chapter 21 verses 1-7 we see Simon Peter and others continuing on with their daily lives, going out to fish.

A Living Sacrifice: Chapter Four

Is this what we would expect, if we are to believe that these men were transformed, simply by the witnessing of their resurrected Lord alone? No, it is not until they receive the gift of the Holy Spirit at Pentecost, and until they were filled with the power of the Holy Spirit. This is when we see Jesus' disciples supernaturally transformed, going out with boldness and with great power, being witnesses for the gospel, and performing miraculous signs and wonders. It was not that the disciples were transformed emotionally or psychologically having seen the risen Lord, but that they were transformed spiritually and supernaturally having received the divine power of God through the baptizing of the Holy Spirit. We see this transformation begin, on the day of Pentecost, when the power of the Holy Spirit came upon the disciples, and to over one hundred believers, as the church was birthed.

> ***When the day of Pentecost came, they were all together in one place. Suddenly a sound like the blowing of a violent wind came from heaven and filled the whole house where they were sitting. They saw what seemed to be tongues of fire that separated and came to rest on each of them. All of them were filled with the Holy Spirit and began to speak in other tongues as the Spirit enabled them.***
> (Acts 2:1-4)

Now some would say that when Jesus told His disciples, that when the Holy Spirit came upon them, that they would receive power, that this power was limited only to the act of being His witnesses and spreading the gospel message with great boldness and courage.

A Living Sacrifice: Chapter Four

This of course, is exactly what we see the disciples Peter and John doing, having been baptized with the Holy Spirit. And we of course know that Jesus told them that they would receive this power to be His witnesses; however, I would suggest to you that although we see evidence of the Spirit's power in the disciple's new found courage and boldness to preach the resurrected Jesus, and to call all men to repent and to be baptized, this does not suggest to say that this is the only purpose of the Holy Spirit and His power in a believer's life. When we look at the totality of Scripture in regards to the person of the Holy Spirit, we see the Spirit's divine power at work, and that His purpose is extremely complex and multifaceted.

The historic and prevailing doctrine of the Christian church, in accordance with the Scriptures, has been that the Holy Spirit is a person distinct from the Father and the Son, though united to both in the mysterious oneness of the Godhead. He is not simply a personification or figurative expression for the divine energy or operation, as some have held at various periods of the history of the church, (Anti-Trinitarians), but He is an intelligent agent, possessed of self-consciousness and freedom. When some think of the Holy Spirit, some might tend to think of the Spirit as simply a force or a power from God, but this denies the Deity of the Holy Spirit, and to have a true biblical understanding of who the Holy Spirit is, we must remember that the Holy Spirit is the third person of the Trinity.

The Holy Spirit is God, just as the Father is God, and Jesus the Son is God. Our relationship with the Holy Spirit is essential if we are to live a life holy and pleasing to God.

Let me digress and take you back now to Ephesians 5:18, **"instead be filled with the Spirit"**. This is the answer to pleasing God and living a holy life. ***Not by might, nor by power, but by my Spirit says the Lord.*** (Zechariah 4:6)

A Living Sacrifice: Chapter Four

We must understand that God Himself indwells you and I, that the Spirit of the living God imparts grace, the power available to us, and that He has spiritually changed you and I and given us new life.

We must understand that God's Spirit alone has given us the ability to know God, to understand and discern the Scriptures, and to empower us to respond in obedience to the commands of Scripture. It is the Spirit Who sanctifies us, makes us holy, teaches us how to pray, and gives us the desire and hunger for prayer and for His Word. It is the Spirit, that leads us, guides us, and directs our every step. When we understand this, then we will know how to please God. It is not in the flesh we please God, nor can we ever do so, it is only in our daily choice to surrender in submission to the Holy Spirit, which then He will empower us to walk according to the spirit. The Holy Spirit covets our obedience, the Spirit wants to fill us, and He will, as we surrender our lives in obedience to Him. Every believer has the Holy Spirit and the power of the Holy Spirit is the same in every believer, but if we are not surrendered to the Holy Spirit then we will be unable to walk in the Spirit's power. As I have already stated, it is not how much of the Holy Spirit a believer has, the question is how much does the Spirit have of the believer? When we are surrendered, we are but empty vessels available and waiting on the Lord to fill us with His Spirit. As we make the choice to surrender to the Holy Spirit, we will begin to live our lives under the influence and the control of the Spirit. There is nothing human about our spiritual lives. Let me say this again, there is nothing human about our spiritual lives, in Christ.

A Living Sacrifice: Chapter Four

In Ezekiel 36:26-27 the LORD says: ***I will give you a new heart and put a new spirit in you; I will remove from you your heart of stone and give you a heart of flesh. And I will put my Spirit in you and move you to follow my decrees and be careful to keep my laws.***

And in 2 Corinthians 5:17, the LORD says: ***Therefore, if anyone is in Christ, he is a new creation; the old has gone, the new has come!***

Now I am not suggesting that in Christ, we are no longer human, but that our human bodies, that God has created, are simply now vessels for God's Spirit to guide, direct, use, and control for His glory. We have already discussed, that we are to offer our bodies as living sacrifices, and this is the very reason that we are commanded by the Scriptures to do so, that we are no longer to live our lives, but that Christ would live through us. Practically speaking, the more we live our lives spiritually minded, the more we will seek after, trust, and ask for the Spirit's power to rule over us. The more we understand our need for the power and purpose of the person of the Holy Spirit in our lives, the more we will learn by the Spirit, that the very reason we draw near to God, through the hearing and the study of His Word, through praise, through prayer, and through fellowship, is for the very purpose of being filled with the Spirit. How do we live lives "*Holy and Pleasing to God?*" By denying self, surrendering to the Holy Spirit, and trusting in God's power alone to move us, and have His way in us.

CHAPTER FIVE:
This Is Your Spiritual Act of Worship.........

What is our spiritual act of worship? In context to Romans 12:1, it is the offering of our bodies as living sacrifices. As I have already discussed, this is a spiritual act, but one that will impact our physical lives. And though we are called to offer our earthly bodies to do the will of God, purposed in good works, the Scriptures also teach that we must be willing and prepared to suffer persecution, and even death for the faith. And so, the Holy Spirit, will not only give the surrendered life the power to do good works, but also give the sacrificed life, the resolve to persevere even through eminent peril and or death. Just as we have witness to the many martyrs in Scripture and throughout history. In this chapter however, although the Apostle Paul is speaking of the offering of our bodies as living sacrifices, as a specific spiritual act, I believe this transcends into all areas of our physical being. Our bodies are not our own, we have been bought at a price, with the precious blood of Jesus, and in 1Corinthians 6:19-20 Paul writes this:

Do you not know that your body is a temple of the Holy Spirit, who is in you, whom you have received from God? You are not your own; you were bought at a price. Therefore honor God with your body.

A Living Sacrifice: Chapter Five

In 1Corinthians 12:12-14, Paul describes the church as a spiritual mechanism. Using a metaphor, Paul describes how our bodies, though one, works together with its many parts, and that so too, does the church. Just as we are each given the same Spirit, each of us are endowed with different gifts, and with many parts, we all make up the body of Christ. **Just as a body, though one, has many parts, but all its many parts form one body, so it is with Christ. For we were all baptized by one Spirit so as to form one body--whether Jews or Gentiles, slave or free--and we were all given the one Spirit to drink. Even so the body is not made up of one part but of many.**

Because we are the church, and each of us, a part of the body of Christ, individually we are not our own, but have been bought at a price. Thus, God wants nothing less from us, than to offer our bodies as an instrument, or a vessel to accomplish His work on earth through us. Everything we say or do accomplished for the glory of God's Kingdom is spiritual, and therefore, it is a spiritual act of worship when we use our bodies, whether in word or in deed, for the glory of God. In Nelson's Illustrated Bible Dictionary the word spiritual is described as being spiritual: *The Christian's every blessing is from the Spirit, as is his understanding of truth. His songs should be sung in the Spirit, and his ability to understand Scripture correctly is given by the Spirit. He is to be so dominated by the Spirit that he can be called spiritual.* This of course is the resounding theme in this book, that as we surrender our bodies as living sacrifices, we can be filled and governed by the Holy Spirit. The Christian life is not one that can be contrived through the acting out of habits, rituals, disciplines or obligations. The Scriptures tell us that we have been **set free** from the regulations and the requirements of the Law and from sin itself. We no longer have to earn a relationship with God through human works, nor was it ever possible for us to do so. We now have His Spirit to enable, guide and govern us.

A Living Sacrifice: Chapter Five

Our worship of God must be void of any human effort and given over to the power of the Holy Spirit. This occurs only through spiritual maturity as we abide in the Lord, and we learn to truly offer our bodies as broken vessels, and seek after the Spirit in all that we do. Jesus speaks of this freedom in John 8:31-32:

To the Jews who had believed him, Jesus said, "If you hold to my teaching, you are really my disciples. Then you will know the truth, and the truth will set you free."

And in Galatians 5:1, it says this: ***It is for freedom that Christ has set us free. Stand firm, then, and do not let yourselves be burdened again by a yoke of slavery.***

As Christians we are commanded to worship God in spirit and in truth, John 4:24 says, **"God is Spirit, and those who worship Him must worship in spirit and in truth."** It is through Christ that we have been born again of the spirit, and are given the Holy Spirit to now enable us to worship God in such a way, both in spirit and in truth. This freedom we have been given, has released us from the power and bondage of sin, and from the regulations and requirements of the Law, and thus now enabling you and I to live in obedience to Christ through His Spirit. If I were to write about this from a historical perspective I would write about the salvation history of the Jew and how the Law relates to the Jew. However, spiritually we are all under the Law, and whether Jew or Gentile, God has placed His Law into our hearts, and though seared into our conscience, we all fall short of living in obedience to the Law.

And when we look at the book of Romans, we see this to be a resounding theme throughout. For one of the Apostle Paul's main points, inspired by the Spirit, is that we are not saved by the Law, but by a righteousness that comes to us all through faith.

For in the gospel a righteousness from God is revealed, a righteousness that is by faith from first to last, just as it is written: "The righteous will live by faith."

A Living Sacrifice: Chapter Five

Now in previous chapters I have discussed how believers have received the righteousness of God through a faith in Jesus, and what this means in terms of our salvation. But now we will see, how this relates to our new found freedom in Christ, to live by the Spirit. The Law was put into place to lead the Jew, as they trusted in the coming Messiah, and ultimately all men to Christ Jesus, Who is the fulfillment of all Messianic prophecy. The Law could never make us righteous, and in fact, this was never the intent of the Law. The Scriptures teach, that the Law was meant to arouse the sinful nature of man, causing man to sin all the more. The intent of the Law then, was actually to show man their inability to keep the Law, and thereby revealing their sinfulness, and thus leading them to Christ.

Romans 3:20, says: **Therefore no one will be declared righteous in his sight by observing the law; rather, through the law we become conscious of sin.** And Galatians 3:23-25, says: **Before this faith came, we were held prisoners by the law, locked up until faith should be revealed. So the law was put in charge to lead us to Christ that we might be justified by faith. Now that faith has come, we are no longer under the supervision of the law.**

Now as we can see, observing the Law in no way has brought about the righteousness of God in sinful man, but we also know that the Law, which are the commandments of God, is of course holy and good, as the Scriptures teach. How then, is this relevant to our ability to worship God, in spirit and in truth? Much in every way!

You see, it is through Christ's sacrifice that the Law was fulfilled and where we find peace with God, and are now able to live by His Spirit. The commandments of the Law have not changed, but we have. In Christ, we are born again of the spirit, the flesh has been crucified, and we now have His righteousness and His Holy Spirit.

What was impossible for you and I to do before, to live in obedience to God's commandments, has now become possible by this spiritual transformation.

A Living Sacrifice: Chapter Five

In Romans 8:1-4, we see this reality revealed through the Scriptures: ***Therefore, there is now no condemnation for those who are in Christ Jesus, because through Christ Jesus the law of the Spirit of life set me free from the law of sin and death. For what the law was powerless to do in that it was weakened by the sinful nature, God did by sending his own Son in the likeness of sinful man to be a sin offering. And so he condemned sin in sinful man, in order that the righteous requirements of the law might be fully met in us, who do not live according to the sinful nature but according to the Spirit.***

In the above passage, Paul is describing the way in which a believer has been transformed from the old self, controlled by the flesh, to the new self, born of the spirit. Romans 6:9-12, helps us to understand this transformation:

For we know that since Christ was raised from the dead, he cannot die again; death no longer has mastery over him. The death he died, he died to sin once for all; but the life he lives, he lives to God. In the same way, count yourselves dead to sin but alive to God in Christ Jesus.

The above passage says, that we are to count ourselves dead to sin, but alive to God in Christ Jesus. What this means, is that the believer is no longer mastered by the power of sin, and that we now have victory over sin, by the Spirit who has transformed us. Before coming to Christ, we were dead in our sin, and could only walk in obedience to the flesh, but even if we were to walk in obedience to the commandments of God in our own effort, this could never make us right with God; in fact, as I have already stated, in the flesh, the commandments of God arouses our sinful desires, which only tempts us to do what is contrary to the commandments of God. It's like when you tell a child, Do Not Touch, it simply arouses their curiosity, and in their sin nature, it compels them to do what they have been told not to do.

A Living Sacrifice: Chapter Five

In Romans 7:19-20, it says this: ***For I do not do the good I want to do, but the evil I do not want to do--this I keep on doing. Now if I do what I do not want to do, it is no longer I who do it, but it is sin living in me that does it.***

As we see in the passage above we are all controlled by the power of sin and our sinful nature, and without the Spirit of God, we are dead in our sin. However, when we come to Christ, we are born of the spirit and transformed from the flesh to the spirit. In this condition, we are released from the regulations and requirements of the Law, the power and bondage of sin, and our sin nature, to now live a life of freedom through the Holy Spirit's power, thus leading to a holy life. Ephesians 2:14-18 says, referring to Christ:

For he himself is our peace, who has made the two one and has destroyed the barrier, the dividing wall of hostility, by abolishing in his flesh the law with its commandments and regulations. His purpose was to create in himself one new man out of the two, thus making peace, and in this one body to reconcile both of them to God through the cross, by which he put to death their hostility. He came and preached peace to you who were far away and peace to those who were near. For through him we both have access to the Father by one Spirit.

The above passage gives us a better understanding as to how we have been transformed spiritually, and It is not by the Law or by anything we could have possibly done. It is only through a faith in Jesus Christ and in Him alone, based upon what He has done. Now having been born again of the spirit we are able to worship God in spirit and in truth. Again, in John 4:23-24 Jesus tells us,

"Yet a time is coming and has now come when the true worshipers will worship the Father in spirit and truth, for they are the kind of worshipers the Father seeks. God is spirit, and his worshipers must worship in spirit and in truth."

A Living Sacrifice: Chapter Five

In John 4:23-24, Jesus is referring to the New Covenant that through Him would come to pass. Again, in Ezekiel 36:26-27, we see the prophecy of the New Covenant proclaimed, where God would make peace with His people through His Spirit:

I will give you a new heart and put a new spirit in you; I will remove from you your heart of stone and give you a heart of flesh. And I will put my Spirit in you and move you to follow my decrees and be careful to keep my laws.

So then, having been spiritually transformed, we worship God in spirit and in truth, by the indwelling of His Spirit. Therefore, as we understand this truth, what exactly then, are our spiritual acts of worship? I believe, our acts of worship can be found in all that we do. Everything we do as believers, with the right spiritual attitude, is for the glory of God, and thus a spiritual act of worship; if in fact, we are being governed by the Spirit. Now to get to this place and to reflect this spiritual mature attitude we must do the ultimate spiritual act of worship, and that is to trust fully in Christ as we abide in Him, offer our bodies as living sacrifices, as we surrender completely, our lives to God. However, once we learn to surrender, and as we understand that it is God who works in us by His Spirit, to will and to act according to His good purpose, we will then learn to seek the Spirit in all that we do. This is what I believe Colossians 3:15-17 is telling us:

Let the peace of Christ rule in your hearts, since as members of one body you were called to peace. And be thankful. Let the word of Christ dwell in you richly as you teach and admonish one another with all wisdom, and as you sing psalms, hymns and spiritual songs with gratitude in your hearts to God. And whatever you do, whether in word or deed, do it all in the name of the Lord Jesus, giving thanks to God the Father through him.

A Living Sacrifice: Chapter Five

Now I would agree, that most believers respond with gratitude and thankfulness in our hearts to God, as Galatians 3:15-17 suggests. And, as we reflect upon our own salvation and how God has saved us through His kindness that has led us to repentance, how could we not love Him and want to worship Him? But we must understand that this attitude does not come from us, but from His Spirit that has transformed us, and that which has produced this desire of worship within us. We could not worship God without His Spirit, nor could we love Him, without the transforming power of His Spirit. ***We love because he first loved us.*** (1John 4:19). My point is, that if we are to do whatever we do, whether in word or deed, all in the name of Jesus, as Colossians 3:15-17 suggests, we must understand, that this could not be possible without the governing of the Holy Spirit. So, when we express to God, a great love and gratitude in our hearts, as we worship Him, in spirit and in truth, it is because of the indwelling of the Spirit. And when we sing psalms, hymns and spiritual songs, if in fact, we are worshipping in spirit and in truth, it is by the Spirit moving in and through us. And when the Word of Christ is dwelling in us richly, again it is because we have His Spirit, because it is only the Spirit that can impart the wisdom of God, into our hearts and minds. Let me give you a practical example of human effort verses true spiritual worship. The Word of God is an accurate historical record therefore, anyone could study and know the Word of God from an intellectual historical perspective. Is the non-believer growing spiritually as he studies the Scriptures? Absolutely not! Why? Because the non-believer does not have the Holy Spirit. However, is the believer who reads or studies the Word of God, but is doing so out of compulsion, obligation, guilt, or habit growing spiritually? Possibly, because in this hypothetical the believer does have the Holy Spirit, and therefore God can move in this person's heart regardless of their spiritual maturity, or motive. But is this believer's study an act of true spiritual worship?

A Living Sacrifice: Chapter Five

I do not believe so, because they are not being led by the Spirit. As we surrender ourselves to God and we seek to be filled with the Spirit, I believe the Spirit will begin to fill us, and lead us into true worship. When we are compelled by the Holy Spirit, not only to study the Scriptures, but in every act of obedience, then that act becomes an act of worship, by the Spirit, and thus accomplished in spirit and in truth. In regards to the study of God's Word, let me quote from the book "<u>Fresh Wind, Fresh Fire</u>" by Jim Cymbala, who quotes William Law, who was an English devotional writer of the early 1700's. He writes: *"Read whatever chapter of Scripture you will, and be ever so delighted with it-yet it will leave you as poor, as empty and unchanged as it found you unless it has turned you wholly and solely to the Spirit of God, and brought you into full union with and dependence upon Him."* I absolutely agree with William Law, and my point well stated. Of course we serve an Awesome Mighty God who can accomplish anything through anyone He wills; however, when we study the totality of Scripture, we see God using men and women surrendered and broken to doing His will, as they are moved and carried along by the Holy Spirit.

That is where God wants you and I. God wants us broken to do His will, and surrendered to His Spirit. Remember, this chapter is about *Your Spiritual Act of Worship,* and the worshiping of God in spirit and in truth. I do not believe we can mature spiritually without the Holy Spirit governing us. In other words we can worship God, and never learn to worship Him in spirit and in truth. Only by the Spirit's dynamic power, can we truly worship God, in spirit and in truth. To give you another practical example, let me discuss an act of worship that is truly dear to my heart, music, and singing psalms, hymns and spiritual songs unto the Lord.

A Living Sacrifice: Chapter Five

    I have been leading others into worship for many years, and my greatest struggle, which became such a heavy burden in my heart, was that I didn't understand why others didn't have the same passion as I did. I am not talking about a passion for music, but a passion for Jesus Christ our Lord, the One worthy of our worship. Why is there such hesitancy on the part of God's people, in the church, to sing and give praise to the Lord? Why are some more passionate about Jesus Christ than others? I understand singing is not natural in the flesh for everyone. However, for the one who has been born again, and who is filled with the Spirit of God, it then becomes natural in his or her spirit, and a joyous experience, and an act of true worship.

    When worshipping the Lord, remains unnatural in a believer, and one is hesitant to raise their hands and their voice to the Lord in praise, the Spirit, I believe, is hindered, quenched or even grieved, in the believer's life. Quite possibly they are simply going through the motions in the flesh, and unfortunately there are many in the church, in this condition. Now this might occur in a believer's life, because the doctrine of the person of the Holy Spirit, is simply not being adequately preached, and people are simply not being adequately discipled, and therefore not growing spiritually, or it might be that the Spirit is being adequately preached, and discipleship is available, but the believer has yet to be broken and surrendered to the Spirit.

    Now, I am not an extreme charismatic believer, there must be order in the church; however, raising your voice loudly and with joy, and raising your hands in humble submission when singing praises to the Lord, this is not charismatic, it is a spiritual act of worship, and one that God is worthy of, and that His Word exhorts!

    Psalm134:1-2 says: ***Praise the LORD, all you servants of the LORD who minister by night in the house of the LORD. Lift up your hands in the sanctuary and praise the LORD.***

A Living Sacrifice: Chapter Five

 I realize we are dealing with millions of believers in the church who are all individuals with different types of personalities, and we all may not be excited about the same things. However, in Christ we are all born again of the same Spirit, and it does not matter if you are an athlete, a housewife, a doctor, a politician, a police officer, an artist, young, or old, when we are walking in the Spirit, governed by the Spirit, and empowered by the Spirit, our personalities will no longer dictate who we are, and our worship will be an act of complete submission as the Spirit compels us to do the will of God, which is to worship Him in spirit and in truth. This of course does not mean that we lose our individuality; however, when our personality dictates how we worship God, or hinders the work of the Holy Spirit in our lives, we are not worshipping God in spirit and in truth, but yielding to the flesh. We need to understand that anything we do as a spiritual act of worship can not come from ourselves, but can only be produced in the power of the Holy Spirit. If we are holding back or hesitant because we're shy or embarrassed we're not in the Spirit. If we hold back, having been gifted, but are modest, this is not humility, but false humility, and we are not in the Spirit. If we do anything from compulsion, guilt, pride, obligation or any motive except to worship God in spirit and in truth, then we are not in the Spirit. The Spirit must dominate the believer to worship God in spirit and in truth. The Spirit must compel you to thirst and hunger for His Word. The Spirit must compel you to prayer. The Spirit must compel you to love. The Spirit must compel you to deny yourself, and the world around you, to now live solely for Christ.

 Now of course, I am not suggesting, that one is not saved because they might lack spiritual fervor or a faith in the power of the Holy Spirit; however, one must be walking in the power of the Holy Spirit to live a life holy and pleasing to God. This is a life surrendered to doing His will, and a life surrendered to doing His will, is a life that has surrendered to His Spirit.

A Living Sacrifice: Chapter Five

    To offer your body as a living sacrifice, and yield your life to the Holy Spirit, *"This is Your Spiritual Act of Worship!"*

    As I end this chapter, I invite you once again, to meditate on the words of *Jesus:*

> ***Then he said to them all: "If anyone would come after me, he must deny himself and take up his cross daily and follow me. For whoever wants to save his life will lose it, but whoever loses his life for me will save it. What good is it for a man to gain the whole world, and yet lose or forfeit his very self?"***
> (Luke 9:23-25)

CHAPTER SIX:

Do Not Conform Any Longer to The Pattern of This World............

The word conform means to act, be in agreement, or comply, and or to act in accordance with current customs or modes. The above exhortation tells us ***not*** to conform and is therefore a commandment, commanding every believer to change the way in which they live by not conforming to the pattern of this world, but trusting now in God's ways. We must understand that when we read such exhortations, we can never change ourselves, it is the Holy Spirit that has transformed us, and as we are governed by the Spirit we will then be able to escape the world's grasp, and its influence over us. It is Jesus Christ, our Lord and Savior, who has overcome the world, and as we abide in Him and are filled with His Spirit we are able to walk in obedience, and it is in Christ's transforming power, that we too have overcome the world. ***For everyone born of God overcomes the world. This is the victory that has overcome the world, even our faith. Who is it that overcomes the world? Only the one who believes that Jesus is the Son of God.*** (1John 5:4-5)

A Living Sacrifice: Chapter Six

Notice that the exhortation tells us **not** to conform **any longer**, which implies that there is a difference between how we used to live and how we are now called to live as believers. The Word of God warns us to turn from the world system, and exhorts us strongly to have no love for the world.

Do not love the world or anything in the world. If anyone loves the world, the love of the Father is not in him. For everything in the world-the cravings of sinful man, the lust of his eyes and the boasting of what he has and does-comes not from the Father but from the world. The world and its desires pass away, but the man who does the will of God lives forever.
(1John 2:15-17)

When the above passage commands us to have no love for the world, God is referring to the world system, and not to those that are in the world. We of course have been commissioned to love those in the world as we love our neighbors as ourselves. The above passage goes on to say that everything in the world system contains the cravings of sinful man; therefore, what we can imply by that, is that the world system is contrary to, and in conflict with, God's moral and sovereign will, and only good for one thing, feeding the flesh, our sinful natures, leading us astray and away from God. As you can see, the world system is closely related to the nature of man; in other words, just as man is sinful, so the world is fallen, and controlled by Satan himself. Ephesians 2:1-2 tells us, that Satan, the ruler of the kingdom of the air, is at the center of our fallen world and the sinful disobedience of man.

As for you, you were dead in your transgressions and sins, in which you used to live when you followed the ways of this world and of the ruler of the kingdom of the air, the spirit who is now at work in those who are disobedient.

A Living Sacrifice: Chapter Six

Now, I could take this opportunity to expound in a very practical way, about the cravings of our sinful natures, the lust of our eyes, and our boasting of our own accomplishments and possessions. But in this chapter I will expound more on how we have been transformed spiritually, which has made us dead to sin and to the world, and alive to Christ, and how we are now set apart for God's glory. With this exhortation, *do not conform to the pattern of this world*, we have looked at what comes first in the Apostle Paul's complete exhortation in Romans 12:1-2, which is to offer our bodies as living sacrifices. We have also looked at the indwelling and the baptism of the Holy Spirit and how the Spirit empowers our lives. I now will attempt to put two and two together. It is in this process of surrendering our lives to God, deciding to deny ourselves, taking up our cross daily and following Jesus, that we will then be in the position to receive the baptism of the Holy Spirit. When we receive the dynamic power of the Spirit, we will then be empowered to live life holy and pleasing to God and for His Kingdom, as we leave the conforming to the pattern of this world behind. Therefore, when we surrender every area of our lives to God, abiding in Jesus, confessing and repenting from our sins, turning from any idol that is weighing us down and hindering our communion with God, and when we ask to be filled with the Holy Spirit and seek to be filled with His dynamic power daily, God will give whatever we ask if we do not doubt, and if it is in accordance with His will. Those that do not believe in the gifts of the Spirit, and doubt in the Holy Spirit's power, will never walk in the Spirit's power!

> *"I have told you these things, so that in me you may have peace. In this world you will have trouble. But take heart! I have overcome the world."*
> (John 16:33)

A Living Sacrifice: Chapter Six

Jesus said that He had overcome the world, and again, if we are abiding in Him, we too have overcome the world, *1John 5:4-5*. Jesus is not saying that by simply believing in Him, that we are made perfect upon belief. We are transformed spiritually, we become a *new creation* in Christ, and we receive His Spirit as a deposit guaranteeing our inheritance, but having been justified, and set free from the power of sin, we are now simply in the right position with God to be sanctified and to grow in Christ. If we never choose to believe in the divine nature, and partake of the Holy Spirit and His power to transform us past our conversion, it will never happen.

Conversion is the beginning, and growing in Christ and maturing in Him takes a deeper surrendering of our lives. It is not that we have been changed physically, but spiritually, and we now have been given the power over the world's influence, over our sinful nature, and over Satan himself, but if we never seek to be filled with the Spirit, we will continue to be influenced, in very subtle ways, by all three. Though we are in Christ, we must choose to be surrendered in obedience to God and seek to be filled with the Holy Spirit. We have overcome the world, and we have been given victory over the world's influence, over our sinful nature, and over Satan himself; however, we must surrender daily to the One who gives us this victory. We must realize, that we grow spiritually, because it is God who is at work in us. It is through the Spirit's power that God produces change in us, and not by us observing special rules or disciplines. While certain disciplines, church attendance, Bible study, prayer and works of service may help us grow, if we are not relying upon the work of the Spirit, they will not.

The Holy Spirit gives Christians great power to live for God, and as many that might believe and mistake walking in the power of the Holy Spirit to be an emotional experience, it is not. We cannot rely upon our feelings or the ebb and flow of emotional highs and lows, as we confuse this with experiencing the power of God.

A Living Sacrifice: Chapter Six

Our feelings are human emotional responses to our circumstances that can easily manipulate us and keep us from truly trusting in the power of God. We see this in the extreme Pentecostal churches, where they not only place an unbiblical emphasis on the Holy Spirit and His gifts, but they rely on human emotion and human experience to bring them into an emotional state of frenzy and euphoria, such as laughing in the spirit, being slain in the spirit, and speaking uncontrollably in tongues. I believe however, when we are truly filled to overflowing with the Holy Spirit's power, we will most likely sense very strongly the presence of God, but it won't be an emotional response, but an attitude, a state of being, and a steadfastness that produces a persistence to live for God that is empowered by the Holy Spirit Himself.

THE POWER OVER SIN AND THE COST OF FOLLOWING JESUS!

The Apostle Paul writes in Galatians 2:20: ***I have been crucified with Christ and I no longer live, but Christ lives in me.*** How was it that Paul could write such a revelation? Of course all Scripture is God breathed and Paul was writing under the Spirit's influence; however, I believe Paul through experience knew exactly what he was writing. Not that Paul had been made perfect and was without sin, but Paul could articulate this revelation because he knew what it meant to be dead to the world and to his sinful nature. Paul knew that just as Christ hung upon the cross lifeless, no longer physically alive to the world, that spiritually Paul too was able to be dead to the world, and to sin. Paul understood that in Christ's death we also die, that is die to the sinful nature, and in His resurrection we now live, that we can now walk, in the power of His Spirit, while all the while, having the hope of eternal life.

A Living Sacrifice: Chapter Six

If we have been united with him like this in his death, we will certainly also be united with him in his resurrection. For we know that our old self was crucified with him so that the body of sin might be done away with, that we should no longer be slaves to sin- because anyone who has died has been freed from sin.
(Romans 6:5-7)

Those who belong to Christ Jesus have crucified the sinful nature with its passions and desires. Since we live by the Spirit, let us keep in step with the Spirit.
(Galatians 5:24-25)

    We are a *new creation* spiritually! In 2Corinthians 5:17 the Scriptures say: **Therefore, if anyone is in Christ, he is a new creation; the old has gone, the new has come!** Although what has taken place spiritually in a believer's life has truly occurred, it is not a transformation that will bear fruit until as believers we act upon the change that has occurred in our heart, mind, and spirit. The sinful nature has been crucified with Christ, and we have the ability to turn from sin and from the world's influence through the power of His Spirit; however, we must learn to surrender in obedience to the Spirit now indwelling us, in order to take hold of the grace of God, as the power of the Spirit then enables us to walk in this newness of life.
    Again, in Luke 9:23-25, Jesus said: **"If anyone would come after me, he must deny himself and take up his cross daily and follow me. For whoever wants to save his life will lose it, but whoever loses his life for me will save it."**
    I have already talked about denying ourselves, and offering our bodies as living sacrifices, and in much the same way, Jesus tells us in the verse above, to lose our lives, to offer our wills, and to live only for Him, regardless of the cost.

A Living Sacrifice: Chapter Six

Tragically, many in the church today are unwilling to live for Jesus in this manner, and many believers in the church are ignorant to His words, and have no spiritual understanding of what it means to count the cost. However, I do not entirely blame individually, those in the body of Christ, as much as I put this responsibility onto the leaders in the church. The leaders in the church are the ones that God has gifted, and has entrusted them with this great responsibility, to lead and disciple those in the body of Christ. Now I do not suggest to say that the leaders in the church are responsible for the individual believer's choices, because there is sin in every church irregardless of the leadership; however, if the leadership denies the power of the Holy Spirit, and the congregation is not properly being fed pure spiritual milk, which eventually will lead to solid spiritual food, and if the multitude is not being discipled, then spiritual growth will lack in the congregation as God's power is quenched. Ultimately, we are all responsible for our own spiritual growth, and the purpose of this book is to spur you on toward a deeper understanding of your relationship with Jesus, and your need for brokenness which leads to the filling of the Holy Spirit; however, it ought to be coming from the pulpits of America as the Word of God is being taught and preached in the power of the Holy Spirit. It is my opinion that we have allowed conformity with the world, and carnality to creep into the church. Here in America we are so desensitized to this subtle evolution that even as you read this opinion, you may be disagreeing with it. If many believers are conformed to the world and are living carnal lives, it is because they are unwilling to abide in Christ, and trust fully in His Word and in His power. But what can we expect from our congregations, if the very people that are expected to lead them, have allowed such secularism and humanism to flow from the pulpit.

A Living Sacrifice: Chapter Six

It doesn't matter what church we attend, or how popular our pastor is, or how well our pastor teaches the Word of God, the influence of the world has crept into the church in America! The influence of our society and the culture within the world we live, should never dictate how we live for God or how the Word of God is preached, but we have allowed it to. Many in the church are offended by the lack of political correctness from the pulpit, and unfortunately many pastors fall into the trap of appeasing these weak minded Christians, rather than being lead by the Spirit, to teach the full counsel of God's Word, in the Spirit's power. Many want to hear feel good stories, as they are satisfied with being stimulated emotionally, as they grow sensationally, but not spiritually.

They want power point presentations to keep them interested, again, as they are appeased and more comfortable with a pastor who tells feel good stories, and who pushes his carnal sense of humor. Now, some pastors may give simple practical teaching to support the application of Scripture, and yet lack any spiritual application, and some simply teach topical sermons, and never open the Word of God. Many pastors deny faith in the gifts of the Holy Spirit and are therefore unable to preach in the Spirit's power. They believe that the Spirit is present and active in a believer's life, but to put any emphasis on the Spirit's power and to teach their congregations that they can actually be empowered in a dynamic way by the filling of the Holy Spirit, is way too charismatic for today. How does the preaching of the Word of God have any power when the one teaching has no faith in the filling of the Holy Spirit! Pastors that teach without the influence and power of the Holy Spirit, teach in their own strength, as they take the control out of God's hands, and into their own, trying to produce something that will last.

A Living Sacrifice: Chapter Six

Of course we know that the root of this problem is man's sinfulness. In the flesh, man tries to do in their own strength, what only God can accomplish through His Spirit. Remember, the flesh profits nothing! I am not implying of course, that every church in America has a pastor that is walking in their own strength; although, all pastor's are men, and all fall short, but in fact there are many great men of faith God has raised up and are walking in the Spirit's power, that are producing much fruit for the Kingdom of God, as they spur on others to walk in step with the Spirit, in much the same way. And as I have already stated, we know that a pastor cannot be held entirely responsible for the individual believer's spiritual growth. Now should a pastor be concerned with the spiritual growth of his flock in which the Lord has entrusted to him? Absolutely! However, although he is faithful in fulfilling his role as he surrenders to the Holy Spirit, it is a given that there is always going to be individual believers in the congregation who are unwilling, or ill-equipped, to do the same. Because a pastor is living his life above reproach and is walking in the Spirit, does not suggest that everyone who has been entrusted to him, is living a surrendered life in the same manner. The *Christian* who is still influenced by the world and who is carnal minded and continuing to conform to the world, is the *Christian* who is not surrendered to the influence of the Spirit, and therefore not conformed to the ways of God. If in fact, we are in Christ, the Spirit will convict us of our sin; however, we will experience a much deeper need for God, as our wills are broken and the Spirit begins to convince us, and empower us, to leave the things of the world behind and surrender to Jesus as Lord of our lives. This reality in a believer's life, in my opinion, is the answer to the believer growing spiritually and living a victorious Christian life. If we are not governed by the Holy Spirit, then we are governed by the sinful nature, the old man who refuses to turn from self and from the influences of the world.

A Living Sacrifice: Chapter Six

We cannot have it both ways, being governed by the flesh our sinful nature, is the opposite of surrendering all to God and trusting solely in Him. Obviously there is always going to be all different levels of individual spiritual growth within the body of Christ; however, my point is that when we remain carnal allowing the world and our own sinful nature to dictate our choices, and how we interpret the worship of God, it can be very subtle and not something we even recognize as sin. We must remember that only God is holy! We will live holy lives conformed to God's ways and dead to sin and to the world, when we learn that the Holy Spirit is God with us, and that it is the Spirit's power that manifests and personifies God's holiness in us and through us, as we surrender to the Spirit. Just as the believer is becoming holy, and as the believer is being made into the image of Christ, this is the work of the Holy Sprit, and as we surrender to God, it is then by His Spirit, that the holiness of God which has been revealed, can now be manifested in us. Let's ponder this, as I take you back to the beginning. Although Adam had free will and was able to choose disobedience, his eyes had not yet been opened to good and evil, until he had sinned. He was created in the image of God, as we all are, but Adam did not have a sin nature. Adam, although having the ability to choose to be disobedient, before he sinned, good was all he knew. God created Adam in His own image to love Him, to worship Him, walk with Him, and live in obedience to Him. And until sin entered the world, that is what Adam did. Again, though Adam was created with free will, he was prone toward holiness because that is how God created him, in His perfect and holy image. Adam was created with great privilege, and with great responsibility to live and move in kingly fashion.

Because Adam sinned however, we are born into sin, and are not prone toward holiness but toward sinfulness, and it took the holiness of God to restore our relationship back with our Creator. And again, it is through Christ we have become the righteousness of God.

A Living Sacrifice: Chapter Six

Once again, 2Corinthians 5:21 tells us: ***God made him who had no sin to be sin for us, so that in him we might become the righteousness of God.***

Let me digress and go back to 1John 2:16: ***For everything in the world-the cravings of sinful man, the lust of his eyes and the boasting of what he has and does-comes not from the Father but from the world.***

This passage is very clear in light of everything I have written. The world represents our hearts, in other words, everything in the world is contrary to God and does nothing, but cultivates and breeds sin. Is this not what the prophet Jeremiah says about our own hearts in Jeremiah 17:9: ***The heart is deceitful above all things and beyond cure. Who can understand it?*** As I look intently at this verse, what I see, tells me that without the righteousness of God through a faith in Jesus Christ, I am the worst of sinners whether I transgress or not. The moment I think I know the limits of my depravity, I read this verse which says: *who can understand*!

Meaning, just when we think we know ourselves, our wicked heart testifies to a state of sinfulness and depravity, to a depth in which we can never even understand. We fall beyond short, we are fallen, period.

As we look again to Psalm 51, doesn't King David in much the same way say the same thing in Psalm 51:3-5?

For I know my transgressions, and my sin is always before me. Against you, you only, have I sinned and done what is evil in your sight, so that you are proved right when you speak and justified when you judge. Surely I was sinful at birth, sinful from the time my mother conceived me.

A Living Sacrifice: Chapter Six

We know that Psalm 51 is known for David's brokenness before the Lord, as he laments over his great sin surrounding Bathsheba; however, David's Psalm is more than simply a confession over sin, but a revelation into deep spiritual truths not only about his own depravity, but also about yours and mine.

If David is saying that his sin is always before him, and that he was sinful at birth, then although he is broken over his sin surrounding Bathsheba, isn't he also then opining that he understands his sin to run deeper than just his transgressions, or the physical acts of adultery and murder? I believe this is exactly what the Lord's inspired Word is revealing through His servant David.

We must understand that this brokenness David reveals in Psalm 51, is deeper than conversion, because of course we know that David was King of Israel, and a man of faith when he sinned. We must also be reminded what God had said about His servant David, that *David was a man after His own heart*, 1Samuel 13:14.

Although many may have a deep conviction of sin at the moment they receive Jesus Christ as Lord and Savior, it is my opinion not one of us knows the depths of our depravity at conversion, thus it is also my opinion that a brokenness that leads to the filling of the Holy Spirit occurs after conversion in a believer's life. If we are truly maturing in Christ, and if we are truly drawing nearer to God in spirit and in truth, then more and more we will come to the realization of our sinfulness and depravity before a holy God.

Brokenness occurs when we truly see ourselves as the sinners we are, and when we truly understand that it is by grace we have been saved. It is my opinion that the sin we commit, even after conversion, is simply the evidence of our depravity, and does not make us any less saved, for it is by **grace** through *faith* in **Christ,** we are set free.

A Living Sacrifice: Chapter Six

However, does this mean we can just sin, and fall back on the grace of God? Absolutely not! But when we do sin, it is the evidence of our depravity and the very reason Christ shed His blood.

And when we look to others, and we are made aware of another believer in sin, this is the evidence of their own depravity, and who are we to condemn, or judge hypocritically, when we are no less sinful and saved by grace and grace alone. Now, I am in no way saying that sin should not be confronted and that there are no consequences for our sin, because as Paul addresses in Romans 5:20-21 and in Romans 6:1-2, though sin might increase grace, this does not give us a license to sin:

5:20-21: ***The law was added so that the trespass might increase. But where sin increased, grace increased all the more, so that, just as sin reigned in death, so also grace might reign through righteousness to bring eternal life through Jesus Christ our Lord.***
6:1-2: ***What shall we say, then? Shall we go on sinning so that grace may increase? By no means! We are those who have died to sin; how can we live in it any longer?***

And so, when I describe sin as the evidence of our depravity, it is not to encourage sin, or to say that we have an excuse for our sinful behavior; however, it is not our transgressions or sinful acts that proves us a sinner. What proves us a sinner, is what God has revealed to us in Jeremiah 17:9, that it is the very condition of our deceitful hearts. Paul writes this, in Romans 7:14-18:

We know that the law is spiritual; but I am unspiritual, sold as a slave to sin. I do not understand what I do. For what I want to do I do not do, but what I hate I do. And if I do what I do not want to do, I agree that the law is good. As it is, it is no longer I myself who do it, but it is sin living in me. For I know that good itself does not dwell in me, that is, in my sinful nature. For I have the desire to do what is good, but I cannot carry it out.

A Living Sacrifice: Chapter Six

Whether we have transgressed or not we are born into sin. This is what is referred to as *"original sin."*

Therefore, just as sin entered the world through one man, and death through sin, and in this way death came to all men, because all sinned-for before the law was given, sin was in the world. But sin is not taken into account when there is no law. Nevertheless, death reigned from the time of Adam to the time of Moses, even over those who did not sin by breaking a command, as did Adam, who was a pattern of the one to come
(Romans 5:12-14)

When Adam sinned, the Scriptures teach that his act of disobedience brought sin into the world and through that sin, death to all. Now this death is both a physical and a spiritual death, and death has come to all, because all are born in sin. This is how you and I are conceived in the womb as David reveals in Psalm 51, *surely I was sinful at birth, sinful from the time my mother conceived me.* When Adam sinned, it was as if all had sinned, and through Adam, all generations were cursed. Therefore, in a way, Adam became man's representative.

And so, when Paul tells us to no longer conform to the pattern of this world, he is telling us that as we offer our lives to the Lord, and surrender our will in obedience to the Lord, in His divine power, we will have the strength, self control and enabling to turn from the world's pattern, as we are renewed in our mind through the Wisdom of God. Before Christ, we were dead in our transgressions, and alive only to our sinful nature, and thus craved and desired the things of the world. However, in Christ, we are dead to sin and to the world, and alive to the spirit, and thus we have been given victory to overcome the sinful nature's passions and desires, and over the influence of the world.

A Living Sacrifice: Chapter Six

Once again, we see this transformation described in Galatians 5:24-26: ***Those who belong to Christ Jesus have crucified the sinful nature with its passions and desires. Since we live by the Spirit, let us keep in step with the Spirit.*** And in Galatians 6:14 Paul writes: ***May I never boast except in the cross of our Lord Jesus Christ, through which the world has been crucified to me, and I to the world.***

In the above Scriptures, as we look closely at them, Paul reveals how those in Christ have been transformed spiritually. Notice Paul says, those who belong to Christ Jesus *have* crucified the sinful nature, and that the world *has been* crucified to us and us to the world. This transformation is a spiritual reality for every believer in Christ. Those in Christ are born again of the spirit, and have been transformed from the flesh to the spirit. This transformation places every believer right with God, but as we are now in the right position with God we must do what Romans 12:1-2 tells us, surrender. As just mentioned, our sinful nature has now been crucified and we are now dead to sin, and what this simply means, is that sin no longer has power over us; however, it is still possible to allow sin to have power over us. Again, Galatians 5:16-18 explains this conflict, and gives us understanding, into how it then becomes possible for the sinful nature to continue to have influence and even control over us, as we deny the Spirit.

So I say, live by the Spirit, and you will not gratify the desires of the sinful nature. For the sinful nature desires what is contrary to the Spirit, and the Spirit what is contrary to the sinful nature. They are in conflict with each other, so that you do not do what you want. But if you are led by the Spirit, you are not under law.

A Living Sacrifice: Chapter Six

If the Apostle Paul exhorts: *"Do Not Conform Any Longer To the Pattern of This World!"* This must mean that conforming is still possible, even in a believer's life, when we are unwilling to surrender our will to the will of God. However, through the Spirit's power and enabling, we have the ability to turn from sin, and the world's influence over our lives, and thus live victoriously for God.

Therefore, we are left with a choice. We can either take hold of the victory we have in Christ, as we surrender our lives to His Spirit, or we can choose to deny the victory, and continue to walk in the flesh. We can fool ourselves, but the Word of God is clear! Without the power of the Holy Spirit, though we may be saved, and though we may have this hope of victory, in the flesh, we will continue to strive hopelessly in our faith, as we conform, and walk influenced, crushed and burdened under the weight of the pattern of this world. In this condition, as we deny the Spirit's power, we will no doubt continue to struggle to know the will of God, and His purpose, and thus live defeated lives for the Kingdom of God, for the flesh will profit nothing.

CHAPTER SEVEN:

But Be Transformed By The Renewing of Your Mind............

In chapter five, I have made brief reference to the Spirit having control over the personality of the believer, and to give an example, you might be a very introverted person, but when you are filled with the Spirit, God can make you bold, because it is not you, but God, who is at work in and through you. In the same way, whatever negative idiosyncrasies you may have in the flesh, they can all be overcome in the Spirit.

Let's look at 2Timothy 1:7 as Paul writes to encourage young Timothy: **For God did not give us a spirit of timidity, but a spirit of power, of love and of self- discipline.**

When we look at Timothy we see a young church leader who was filled with the Holy Spirit, and imparted with the spiritual gifts necessary to accomplish the work of God.

A Living Sacrifice: Chapter Seven

Now Timothy, no different than ourselves, had to continue to fan into flame these gifts and seek the Spirit for boldness, strength and self-discipline. Paul again, encourages Timothy in 1Timothy 4:11-12:

Command and teach these things. Don't let anyone look down on you because you are young, but set an example for the believers in speech, in life, in love, in faith and in purity.

We know that Timothy was young and was faced with much adversity as he stood up against the false teachers that had arisen in the church at Ephesus. Now I do not believe it was Timothy's forceful personality or dynamic human ability that gave him the resolve to remain faithful to the ministry. I believe it was the Holy Spirit and the gifts imparted to him by the Spirit that gave him his resolve, and ability, despite his youth, and his most likely timid personality. In this chapter we will look at being renewed in our minds and what exactly it is that renews us. God wants to accomplish change in us, and mold us into who He wants us to be for His purpose and His glory. As believers we must learn to find our identity in Christ and set aside the desire to find our identity in the world or in our ego. This does not mean that as human beings we lose our individuality; however, we are now to be controlled and governed by the Spirit, and not by our old nature, which includes both our negative and what we might think are positive personality traits, that in Christ, have been crucified and renewed by the Spirit.

This chapter is also related to chapter 6 as the Apostle Paul exhorts us to no longer conform to the world, because it is the world that influences and shapes our sinful nature. It is God however, who transforms us spiritually and has put His Spirit in us, that we might deny ourselves, the flesh, and now choose to live by His Spirit.

A Living Sacrifice: Chapter Seven

Ezekiel 36:27 says: *"And I will put my Spirit in you and move you to follow my decrees and be careful to keep my laws."*

In Ezekiel, it tells us that God has put His Spirit in us and that His Spirit will move us to follow His ways. It is therefore the Spirit of God who transforms us, but how? God uses His Law, or His Word. The Holy Spirit renews our minds with the Word of God.

As the Word of God is taught and studied, the Holy Spirit imparts us with the Wisdom of God, and the ability to discern His Word. We then are equipped and enabled to live out God's knowledge in our lives. But we must remember, even having been equipped and enabled by God's Spirit, we must always rely upon the direction and guidance of the Holy Spirit. We can not assume that in our new found freedom in Christ, that we can now just go off in our own direction. So let me make one thing clear from the outset, we can not be transformed or renewed in our mind without the power of the Holy Spirit. One can not even discern the Scriptures without the Spirit, and we see this truth revealed in 1Corinthians 2:12-16:

> ***We have not received the spirit of the world but the Spirit who is from God, that we may understand what God has freely given us. This is what we speak, not in words taught us by human wisdom but in words taught by the Spirit, expressing spiritual truths in spiritual words. The man without the Spirit does not accept the things that come from the Spirit of God, for they are foolishness to him, and he cannot understand them, because they are spiritually discerned. The spiritual man makes judgments about all things, but he himself is not subject to any man's judgment: "For who has known the mind of the Lord that he may instruct him?" But we have the mind of Christ.***

A Living Sacrifice: Chapter Seven

Of course we know that those that are not born again of the spirit, do not have the Holy Spirit; however, is it possible for a believer to have the Spirit and still lack discernment? Absolutely! This is why Paul is exhorting us to be transformed by the renewing of our minds, and this can only occur through the Wisdom found in God's Word. If this transforming took place by osmosis, through simply having been born again of the spirit, then Paul's exhortation would not be necessary. We must first understand that the renewing of our minds can only come through God's Word, and more importantly that this can only occur through the Holy Spirit imparting our minds with understanding. When we were in the world, we knew only the views and ideologies taught by the world, and lived only according to our nature which was contrary to God. Now growing up, we most likely were taught morals, values, and principles which prompted us to conduct ourselves decently; however, what our parents taught us did not change our heart, mind or spirit, nor give us the ability to live in obedience to God. In fact, until we were born of the spirit, it didn't matter how good we think we were, in reality we were controlled by the sinful nature and the world's influence, which is every non-believer's stronghold. Our minds were filled only with carnal and worldly knowledge, and unconsciously, within our spiritually dead souls, this dictated how we lived our lives. How is it then, that all that we have become through the world's influence, are we changed? It is through the renewing of our minds, which changes our hearts, and how we view the world, how we view ourselves, and how we now view God and His ways. Our very faith comes by hearing and hearing by the word of God, and that the fear of the LORD is the beginning of knowledge. God also tells us that fools despise wisdom and instruction, and until we grow in this truth, and in the knowledge of our Lord and Savior Jesus Christ we will continue being influenced by worldly philosophies, which are in conflict with the Wisdom of God.

A Living Sacrifice: Chapter Seven

It is God's Word, His Wisdom, and God Himself that changes and renews the mind of the believer by His Spirit. We need to be renewed in our minds, as we allow the Holy Spirit to wash and cleanse us of our carnal worldly knowledge, that has set itself up against God, and that has influenced, dictated, and controlled all of our carnal thoughts, behaviors, and attitudes.

We must now, surrender to the Spirit, as we allow the wisdom of God, to renew our minds, as our thoughts, behaviors, and attitudes, then begin to reflect the character of God. We must learn to surrender the natural mind to the Spirit, Whom has transformed us into a new creation, and has imparted us with the mind of Christ. In Isaiah 55:6-9 God reveals how we are not like Him, that He is God and we are not, and that He is greater than you and I.

Seek the LORD while he may be found; call on him while he is near. Let the wicked forsake his way and the evil man his thoughts. Let him turn to the LORD, and he will have mercy on him, and to our God, for he will freely pardon. "For my thoughts are not your thoughts, neither are your ways my ways," declares the LORD. "As the heavens are higher than the earth, so are my ways higher than your ways and my thoughts than your thoughts.

Now in 1Corinthians 2:11-13 we are given insight as to how we can have understanding into what God has revealed, and it is by His Spirit:

For who among men knows the thoughts of a man except the man's spirit within him? In the same way no one knows the thoughts of God except the Spirit of God. We have not received the spirit of the world but the Spirit who is from God, that we may understand what God has freely given us. This is what we speak, not in words taught us by human wisdom but in words taught by the Spirit, expressing spiritual truths in spiritual words.

A Living Sacrifice: Chapter Seven

And it is in Isaiah 40:13-14 where we are told of God's omniscience, His superior knowledge and wisdom, and His power to know all things. Our understanding is futile compared to the all surpassing wisdom and knowledge of our Creator.

Who has understood the mind of the LORD, or instructed him as his counselor? Whom did the LORD consult to enlighten him, and who taught him the right way? Who was it that taught him knowledge or showed him the path of understanding?

And again, in 1Corinthians 2:15-16, as we have learned that only through the Spirit do we understand Spiritual truth, it is also through the Spirit that we who are spiritual are able to judge all things as we have been given the mind of Christ Jesus.

The spiritual man makes judgments about all things, but he himself is not subject to any man's judgment: "For who has known the mind of the Lord that he may instruct him?" But we have the mind of Christ.
(1Corinthians 2:15-16)

Having the mind of Christ through the Spirit, is a spiritual transformation and a reality for every believer, and being renewed in our minds through the Word of God is the work of the Spirit. In James 3:13-14 however, God reveals that in man's sinfulness, wisdom becomes corrupted, and leads to the denying of truth. Such wisdom is not from God, and not from heaven but is earthly, unspiritual and of the devil. Trusting in the wisdom of man is where we will find disorder, and every evil practice. In contrast however, the man having the mind of Christ is able to discern God's truth which is pure, spiritual and filled with His wisdom, which flows from heaven.

A Living Sacrifice: Chapter Seven

James 3:13-4:1 says: *Who is wise and understanding among you? Let him show it by his good life, by deeds done in the humility that comes from wisdom. But if you harbor bitter envy and selfish ambition in your hearts, do not boast about it or deny the truth. Such "wisdom" does not come down from heaven but is earthly, unspiritual, of the devil. For where you have envy and selfish ambition, there you find disorder and every evil practice. But the wisdom that comes from heaven is first of all pure; then peace-loving, considerate, submissive, full of mercy and good fruit, impartial and sincere. Peacemakers who sow in peace raise a harvest of righteousness.*

DO NOT LEAN ON YOUR OWN UNDERSTANDING

In Proverbs 3:5-8 it says this: *Trust in the LORD with all your heart and lean not on your own understanding; in all your ways acknowledge him, and he will make your paths straight. Do not be wise in your own eyes; fear the LORD and shun evil. This will bring health to your body and nourishment to your bones.*

Do not lean on your own understanding? How is this even possible, you might ask? Well, all things are possible through Christ who strengthens us, and Jesus Himself said that you can do nothing without Him, and so as the proverb begins, you must trust in the Lord with all your heart. We need the Spirit's enabling as we seek to be renewed in our minds through the full counsel of God's Word.

Our minds are finite and the mind of Christ is of course infinite. When we try to even begin to fathom the things of God, His eternal existence, His Sovereignty and His Majesty, when left to our own understanding, it can actually make our brains hurt; however, when we acknowledge the greatness of our God, and we realize our own insignificance, we begin to understand God is God and we are not. Therefore, that being said, doesn't it make sense that God should be the one in control?

A Living Sacrifice: Chapter Seven

If God is in control, and if He in fact is sovereign, how is it then that He communicates His sovereignty over us? It is through His Word, where knowledge, wisdom, and understanding avail. Apart from general revelation, God reveling Himself through, what I like to call the three C's, **Creation**, our **Conscience**, and His Son Jesus **Christ,** everything that is known about God is revealed through His Word. Tough given a conscience and God putting His Law in our hearts, there is no commandment, statute or decree that reveals God's moral will apart from His Word, and regardless of what we know of God's character, His sovereign and moral will, and His eternal plan, they have all been revealed to us, and confirmed through His Word, and by His Spirit. What does the Bible have to say about the human mind, and the commandments surrounding our instruction to leave behind the wisdom of man and cleave to the wisdom of God? Well, let us begin with the spiritual transformation that has occurred inwardly as believers, and what gives us this new found ability to turn from the old man controlled by the sinful nature, and as it relates to our minds, the ability we now have to live by the Spirit. Jesus said, in Luke 10:27: He answered:

"Love the Lord your God with all your heart and with all your soul and with all your strength and with all your (mind), and, 'Love your neighbor as yourself." (emphasis added).

In the above passage, much in the same way as Paul, Jesus is first to exhort us to lay down our bodies as living sacrifices, as He commands us to love God with our entire being. Believers need to understand that in Christ, just as our heart is transformed, and our spirit is transformed, so too is our mind. We must understand that our minds are the key to our relationship with God. Everything we think, say, and do, flows first through our minds. All wisdom and knowledge that affects our inner being, must first flow inwardly through our minds and into our hearts.

A Living Sacrifice: Chapter Seven

This is as true for the one spiritually dead as it is for the one who has been born again; however, it is only those who have been born of the spirit who have escaped the corruption of this world, and the sinful nature. Again, we see this in Romans 8:5-11:

Those who live according to the sinful nature have their minds set on what that nature desires; but those who live in accordance with the Spirit have their minds set on what the Spirit desires. The mind of sinful man is death, but the mind controlled by the Spirit is life and peace; the sinful mind is hostile to God. It does not submit to God's law, nor can it do so. Those controlled by the sinful nature cannot please God. You, however, are controlled not by the sinful nature but by the Spirit, if the Spirit of God lives in you. And if anyone does not have the Spirit of Christ, he does not belong to Christ. But if Christ is in you, your body is dead because of sin, yet your spirit is alive because of righteousness. And if the Spirit of him who raised Jesus from the dead is living in you, he who raised Christ from the dead will also give life to your mortal bodies through his Spirit, who lives in you.

In Romans Chapter 8, Paul expounds upon the difference between the one living according to the sinful nature having their mind set on what the sinful nature desires, and the one who is living according to the spirit, having their mind set on what the Spirit desires. Before believing, our minds were set on what the sinful nature desires; however, once having been born again of the spirit, in Christ, we now are no longer controlled by the sinful nature, but by the Spirit. Notice that Paul writes that you, (the believer), however, are controlled not by the sinful nature, but by the Spirit, if the Spirit of God lives in you.

A Living Sacrifice: Chapter Seven

Remember, upon believing in Christ we were transformed from the realm of the flesh to the realm of the spirit. This is a spiritual reality for every believer; however, our very beings which includes the mind, has now become a battlefield, and although transformed into a *new creation,* this battle between the flesh and the spirit has begun and will continue on, until we enter eternity. Satan, of course knows this, and he also knows our flesh is weak, and so to get us to fall, he attempts to tempt us with his schemes, and by using his arsenal of weapons, he attacks the mind of the believer.

Satan knows, that through the mind of the believer, is where our sinful nature is aroused, which then causes our deceitful hearts to conceive sin. That is why, if we are not fitted with the full armor of God, (Ephesians 6:10-18), and our minds are not set on what the Spirit desires, we will loose this battle and Satan will accomplish exactly what he has set out to do, and that is to make us ineffective for the Kingdom of God. This is where the renewing of our minds comes into play. Remember what I said about our minds being the key to our relationship with God? I say this, because it is what we allow to enter our minds that will affect our entire being, and this will determine our effectiveness to live for God. As believers, do we remain in the futility of our own understanding and knowledge, as we set our minds on the world, and on our carnal and sinful desires? Or do we surrender, allowing are minds to be renewed, as we then set our minds on what the Spirit desires? Much in the same way Paul writes to believers in Romans 8, in Ephesians 4:20-24, we see how God reveals to us how we should now live: ***You, however, did not come to know Christ that way. Surely you heard of him and were taught in him in accordance with the truth that is in Jesus. You were taught, with regard to your former way of life, to put off your old self, which is being corrupted by its deceitful desires; to be made new in the attitude of your minds; and to put on the new self, created to be like God in true righteousness and holiness.***

A Living Sacrifice: Chapter Seven

As it says in Ephesians 4:20-24, if we put off the old self which is being corrupted by its deceitful desires, and instead be made new in the attitude of our minds, as we put on the new self, created to be like God, it implies then, we will live the holy life we have been called to live. But, how are we made new in the attitude of our minds? We are renewed in the attitude of our minds through the Word of God, as the Spirit imparts God's Wisdom, into our minds and into our hearts. Many Christians believe, mainly because they are not spiritually minded, which can only be produced by the Spirit, that the Word of God is to be studied deeply by pastors, scholars, and teachers, but not by every believer. Many might have the understanding, that it is the responsibility of their pastor to feed them the Word of God, and it is, but God does not intend for the believer to be renewed solely by others, remember, we have a personal relationship with God the Father, with His Son Jesus Christ, and with the Holy Spirit. We cultivate communion and fellowship with God by spending personal time with Him. Those who do not, in my opinion, simply have not surrendered their lives to the Spirit, and because of this, they are weak minded Christians who hinder and quench the work of the Holy Spirit in their lives. Now God has not called every believer to teach, in fact, in Ephesians chapter 4 it tells us, that God has called some to be apostles, some to be prophets, some to be evangelists, and some to be pastors and teachers, and in James chapter 3 the Scriptures warn those that would aspire to be teachers, that not many should presume to be teachers, because those who teach will be judged more strictly. This ought to cause anyone in the faith to seek the will of God earnestly before jumping into something that might bring judgment upon themselves; however, this chapter is not about becoming a pastor or a teacher, but about becoming sanctified and renewed in your mind, that you might live a life according to the will of God, as you walk in, and pursue holiness in your life.

A Living Sacrifice: Chapter Seven

    I would expect and hope that if one is a teacher or a pastor, that they are walking in the power of the Spirit, and are being daily renewed in their mind, by the Spirit, through the Wisdom of God. Certainly pastors and teachers, and evangelists have a duty to diligently study the Scriptures, but if any believer is to grow in their faith and live a life faithful to God's calling, they also must be transformed by the renewing of their minds, through the study of God's Word. Throughout the Psalms we find many passages of Scripture that speak of the majesty and the flawlessness of God's Word.

> ***As for God, his way is perfect; the word of the LORD is flawless. He is a shield for all who take refuge in him,***
> (Psalm 18:30)

    As we look into God's perfect law we find His perfect will being revealed. And again, in Psalm 119 we find the moral will of God revealed, and that the goal for every believer is to live in obedience to God, by living according to His Word.

> ***How can a young man keep his way pure? By living according to your word. I seek you with all my heart; do not let me stray from your commands. I have hidden your word in my heart that I might not sin against you. Praise be to you, O LORD; teach me your decrees. With my lips I recount all the laws that come from your mouth. I rejoice in following your statutes as one rejoices in great riches. I meditate on your precepts and consider your ways. I delight in your decrees; I will not neglect your word.***
> (Ps 119:9-16)

A Living Sacrifice: Chapter Seven

To know God's moral will for our lives we must study His Word, and know the Scriptures. The Holy Spirit will guide us through the Scriptures and enable us to not only discern the Scriptures, but will write them on our hearts, and with the Spirit's power we will walk in the light of God's Word. Psalm 119:105 tells us: **God's Word is a lamp to our feet and a light to our path.** It is God's Word that illuminates our path, and it is God Himself who will make our paths straight, as we follow the light that lights our path. This chapter is not about obeying God's Word, this chapter is about knowing God's Word, for how can we live in obedience to God, if we are ignorant to His moral will, which is revealed only through the Scriptures? But it is more than that, we must also know, the character of God, His sovereign will, and His eternal plan, and understanding to the extent God has revealed these truths, is found only in His Word. It is the work of the Holy Spirit alone, that imparts this wisdom to all believers. Is there more to the renewing of our minds than the wisdom found in God's Word, where we find His character, His sovereign and moral will, and His eternal plan revealed? Some would say yes, but I would agree to disagree, let me explain. Philosophy has been around for thousands of years, and false teachings were rampant in the first century.

We may not all know the philosophical views of Aristotle, Socrates or Plato, but we most certainly have heard of these infamous philosophers, and no doubt have been influenced by their world views. The word philosophy comes from the Greek words **Phileo,** which means "love" and **Sophia,** which means "wisdom", and so it is the love of wisdom that motivates the philosopher. Very simply, philosophy is the examination of the convictions by which people live their lives in order that the philosopher might establish a consistent way of life as evidence for their own expressed world view.

A Living Sacrifice: Chapter Seven

However, the world view of the philosopher, is just that, a world view, and although it may reflect a general knowledge of God, and express the same convictions of those who know God, it is based upon worldly wisdom. We see in 1Corinthians 3:18-20, that the wisdom of man is foolishness in God's sight:

Do not deceive yourselves. If any one of you thinks he is wise by the standards of this age, he should become a "fool" so that he may become wise. For the wisdom of this world is foolishness in God's sight. As it is written: "He catches the wise in their craftiness"; and again, "The Lord knows that the thoughts of the wise are futile."

In Colossians 2:8 the Scriptures warn us not to rely upon the philosophy according to man's wisdom, but to rely solely on the wisdom of God, that is in Christ Jesus: ***See to it that no one takes you captive through hollow and deceptive philosophy, which depends on human tradition and the basic principles of this world rather than on Christ.*** To give an example: Gnosticism, which scholars believe began toward the end of the first century or possibly in the second, is an esoteric religious philosophy which stressed knowledge as the way to God. But as we can see in the above passages, wisdom from man is deceptive, and is of the world and foolishness in the sight of God. You can see then how we might be deceived by the enemy if we are not grounded in the truth, the wisdom found in God's Word. Again, because a philosophical world view is based upon a general revelation of God, that might express convictions based upon what is moral, and because what is moral ultimately, as we know, comes from a holy God, we can be easily entangled by a hollow philosophy which is nothing more than a counterfeit for God's Wisdom; however, philosophy is a world view and is not centered in Christ and therefore, it is not the Wisdom of God.

A Living Sacrifice: Chapter Seven

The wisdom of man is nothing more than humanism, secularism, and hollow philosophy. So how do we fight against this philosophy from man, the wisdom of this age? In 2Corinthians 10:3-6 we find the answer to this question:

For though we live in the world, we do not wage war as the world does. The weapons we fight with are not the weapons of the world. On the contrary, they have divine power to demolish strongholds. We demolish arguments and every pretension that sets itself up against the knowledge of God, and we take captive every thought to make it obedient to Christ. And we will be ready to punish every act of disobedience, once your obedience is complete.

As I have already written, it is the mind where Satan will try and wage war, thus it is the mind that we must allow the Spirit to transform and renew. For just as Satan's attacks are spiritual, so too are our defenses against his schemes. We have divine power to demolish strongholds, and this power comes from the Spirit as we rely on the Spirit to transform us by the renewing of our minds through the study of God's Word. We take captive every thought to make it obedient to Christ, only when we are renewed in our minds with the Wisdom of God, and only then can His knowledge then be applied in our lives. Now that I have brought up human philosophy, even in the Christian faith, there is an area of study that concerns me, and one which I am well studied, and it is known as the study of Apologetics. We derive this word, *Apologetics*, from the Scriptures, found in 1 Peter 3:15:

But in your hearts set apart Christ as Lord. Always be prepared to give an answer to everyone who asks you to give the reason for the hope that you have. But do this with gentleness and respect.

A Living Sacrifice: Chapter Seven

The Greek word for *answer*, in 1Peter 3:15, is **apologia.** Apologia means a reason or a defense, if you will. We ought to have a reason, and or a defense for the Christian faith; however, the study of Apologetics, in my opinion, can be very dangerous, especially to the new believer. To the carnal mind, it can easily fall into the category of human philosophy. Please do not misunderstand me, I believe that Christians should not have a blind faith, and there is a time and place for the believer to be encouraged and edified by the evidences for God and the reliability of the Scriptures; however, do we truly need to go outside of the Scriptures to defend the faith? I believe the Scriptures tell us that we are not only to rely upon the Holy Spirit to transform us through the renewing of our minds through God's Word, but also to speak through us, the wisdom of God. I believe it is the Spirit that prepares our hearts to give an answer to everyone who asks us to give the reason for the hope that we have, and also to speak boldly when the opportunities to defend the faith present themselves. In Acts 6:8-10, we see Stephen being verbally attacked by the Jews in the Synagogue of the Freedmen, and when the opposition arose, the men began to argue with Stephen about the faith, and in verse 6:10 it says this: **but they could not stand up against his wisdom or the Spirit by whom he spoke.**
And if we look back, to the beginning of the passage, in Acts 6:8, it says this: **Now Stephen, a man full of God's grace and power.**

Stephen was a man filled with the Spirit of God, and it would seem, that the church of the twenty first century seems to think we need something more than God's grace and power. We have gotten so far off the mark that it seems some would believe God's Wisdom is not found solely in His Word, but also in our own innovative ideas as well. Some might think that if we become more intellectual through religious avenues such as Apologetics, that this somehow is equivalent to growing spiritually in the Spirit's power through God's Word.

A Living Sacrifice: Chapter Seven

    I am not suggesting, that the study of Apologetics is wrong or evil. My point is however, it can be nothing more than hollow philosophy to the believer who is not relying upon the Spirit of God to renew his or her mind, through the Word of God, but instead allowing themselves to get lost in outside studies, as these studies then take the place of growing in the Wisdom of God. We can get so caught up in defending the faith that our minds are focused on the means for the defense, and taken off of Christ the Author and perfecter of our faith. When seeking wisdom and knowledge we can tend to believe that because the outside sources we are studying, are relating to the things of God, such as Apologetics, that these studies are automatically beneficial and edifying; however, it can be just as detrimental, if we are allowing these outside studies to take the place of growing in the wisdom and knowledge of God, through His Word and by His Spirit. Within the proper context, and based upon the maturity of the believer, outside studies that expound upon the Wisdom of God, should accomplish one thing, and that is to move you to seek after the Spirit, and only the wisdom revealed in God's Word. When it is not the Holy Spirit moving us, and He is not active in our studies, then more than likely, we are simply being puffed up with knowledge, as we grow very little spiritually. Intellectual knowledge is unspiritual, and will soon show itself to be futile and quite possibly detrimental, as our pride becomes a stumbling block. We see this in 1Corinthians 8:1b-2: ***Knowledge puffs up, but love builds up. The man who thinks he knows something does not yet know as he ought to know. But the man who loves God is known by God.***

    The above passage is admittedly taken out of context; however, it is very clear in communicating, that it is contrary to God, for man to rely upon his own knowledge gained through the world and his own life experience, rather than on the knowledge of God, gained through His Word, imparted by His Spirit.

A Living Sacrifice: Chapter Seven

When we live such surrendered lives, that it becomes the Spirit and the Spirit alone governing our lives, only then can our minds be renewed, and our minds then be set on what the Spirit desires. We cannot be renewed partially, in other words, we cannot just go to church and learn the things of God, and then try by our own best effort and understanding, to simply apply the practical teachings of Scripture to our lives. When we live in such a way, we deny the power of the Holy Spirit and take the holiness of God, and the sanctifying work of the Spirit into our own hands. If we could motivate ourselves to live in obedience to God, then why is it that we need to be born again? We are a *new creation* in Christ not simply to benefit from the blessings of God, or reap the reward of eternal life, but God gives us this newness of life, because we are unable to have fellowship and communion with God and enter into His Kingdom without first becoming holy. Becoming righteous in His sight is the only way that God could look upon you and I with forgiveness, and to not treat us as our sins deserve. Again, this righteousness is not something we earn, but is a righteousness from God, imparted to us through Christ. For it is Christ who is righteous and it is Christ who now dwells in you and me, through His Spirit. Therefore, just as righteousness is not our own, and cannot be worked out by human effort, we too are incapable of living holy lives through working out practical life choices by human effort. This is what I believe Paul is exhorting in Romans chapter 8. When we live according to the flesh, our minds are set on what the sinful nature desires, but when we live according to the spirit our minds are set on what the Spirit desires. However, to live according to the spirit, we must surrender to the Holy Spirit now at work in us, and seek to be filled with His power to govern us. We might believe that we are righteous as we are outwardly living a good and pleasing life, doing the right things, and making all the right choices, but if this is not produced by the Spirit, then it is of the flesh, and will profit nothing.

A Living Sacrifice: Chapter Seven

Meaning, I believe that sin is not just disobedience, but it can also be walking in obedience by our own human effort, because in both we are denying God and turning from our trust and faith in Him. Therefore, part of the renewing of our minds, is the spiritual attitude, (based upon the Scriptures), that leads us to the understanding, that without the Spirit governing us, and unless the Spirit is the One moving us, we will never have victory over the flesh. So again, Paul exhorts, *"Be Transformed by The Renewing of Your Mind!"* When this begins to occur, through the power of the Holy Spirit, I believe as a *new creation* in Christ, our attitudes will begin to turn slowly toward the spiritual, where the will of God is manifested. Faith is what facilitates all spiritual transformation, and so we must first believe in the filling of the Holy Spirit, the spiritual gifts the Spirit imparts, and the power of God that empowers all believers to live the dynamic lives God has ordained. We will have the attitude of Christ, when we surrender to the Spirit, having been given the mind of Christ. Loving the Lord our God, with all our minds, requires faith and surrender. Once having come to Christ as Savior, we must now surrender to Christ as Lord; however, sowing to the flesh will keep us from being completely governed by the Spirit, and in our minds, is where it all begins. We will live by the Spirit, and our minds will be set on what the Spirit desires, when we surrender to the Spirit, as we leave no provision for the flesh. In Ephesians 1:17-20, Paul prays for wisdom for the church: ***I keep asking that the God of our Lord Jesus Christ, the glorious Father, may give you the Spirit of wisdom and revelation, so that you may know him better. I pray that the eyes of your heart may be enlightened in order that you may know the hope to which he has called you, the riches of his glorious inheritance in his holy people, and his incomparably great power for us who believe. That power is the same as the mighty strength he exerted when he raised Christ from the dead and seated him at his right hand in the heavenly realms.***

CHAPTER EIGHT:

Then You Will Be Able to Test and Approve What God's Will Is..............

What is God's will for my life? This question is often asked, and many attempt, from a practical perspective, to give the answer to this question. We live in a post first century era, where the church began trusting in the direction, governing and control of the Holy Spirit. God's will is revealed and accomplished in the church, by God's power, through God's people. It is my opinion however, that the church has fallen away from believing that God actually intervenes in human history to accomplish His sovereign plan, in the same way today, as He did in the first century, and as He has always throughout human and salvation history. We may not necessarily see the miraculous and all the signs and wonders, but God is unchanging, **Jesus Christ is the same yesterday and today and forever.**

A Living Sacrifice: Chapter Eight

When a believer walks in the Spirit and expresses a mature spiritual attitude, their faith in the person and purpose of the Holy Spirit, might seem by some in the church to be overly charismatic, or that they are too spiritually minded, or worse, they might even be accused of being spiritually prideful.

But this again, is the resounding theme throughout this entire book. Because God Himself indwells every believer, we are more than human, we are **spiritual**, and we are a **"new creation,"** thus our perspective ought to be in line with the Spirit, and not in line with carnality, (our own human understanding), or the world, where the flesh operates. Now when speaking of God's will, there are really two different realities we must look at. We know that God calls us to be holy, to obey His commandments and to follow Him all the days of our lives. This of course, is God's will, but what about the works that God has predestined for you and I to walk in? What about how God has already decided and predestined how it is He is going to use you and I for His kingdom? This chapter is not about answering what God's will is for your life, that is not the right question, this chapter is about what God's will is period. How God wants to use us has already been determined, and is His business not ours, revealed in His timing, and only to those who surrender to doing His will.

When we believe God's will is about our own personal business, we then will choose our own path, as we rubber-stamp our own plans, as we seek the Lord's blessing. Jesus went to the cross, obeying the Father, to do the will of God, and even Christ Himself was filled with the Spirit of God, as He freely laid down His life. As Jesus died for the sins of the world, He was accomplishing God's will, as He fulfilled the Scriptures. Have you gone to the cross? That is God's will, that you surrender all in obedience, at the cross!

If your faith in Jesus Christ has been nothing more than a mere human experience, then I would encourage you to surrender, that you might experience the spiritual.

A Living Sacrifice: Chapter Eight

When contemplating the will of God you must be willing to seek the Living Water, the Holy Spirit, to fill you, so that God's will might be found in this torrent of Living Water as it flows forth in and through you. Experiencing God's will is found only through the dying of self, and seeking to be filled with His Spirit. Only God knows the answer to questions concerning His will, in regards to our earthly existence, because it is God who has already predestined, and ordained our lives for every good work. The will of God can only truly be revealed and accomplished through His Holy Spirit. Now sure, we are intellectual beings, and we can sit around and try and figure out God's will for our lives, or we can seek God and trust and believe in the power of the Holy Spirit. As we walk in the Spirit, and are filled, we will begin to live in obedience to the Spirit, as the Spirit then, will begin to govern our lives.

It is God who knows His will for your life, and His Spirit who will reveal it to you. It is the Holy Spirit that will give you the spiritual gifts and His power to fulfill the works prepared in advance for you to walk in, and it is the Holy Spirit, if governing your life, that will guide and direct your every step in fulfilling and accomplishing the will of God in your life. I encourage you to look intently at the following verses, seek the Spirit, and ask the LORD to speak to your heart.

> *For you created my inmost being; you knit me together in my mother's womb. I praise you because I am fearfully and wonderfully made; your works are wonderful, I know that full well. My frame was not hidden from you when I was made in the secret place. When I was woven together in the depths of the earth, your eyes saw my unformed body. All the days ordained for me were written in your book before one of them came to be.*
> (Psalm 139:13-16)

A Living Sacrifice: Chapter Eight

The word of the LORD came to me, saying, "Before I formed you in the womb I knew you, before you were born I set you apart; I appointed you as a prophet to the nations." "Ah, Sovereign LORD," I said, "I do not know how to speak; I am only a child." But the LORD said to me, "Do not say, 'I am only a child.' You must go to everyone I send you to and say whatever I command you. Do not be afraid of them, for I am with you and will rescue you," declares the LORD.
(Jeremiah 1:4-8)

"For I know the plans I have for you," declares the LORD, "plans to prosper you and not to harm you, plans to give you hope and a future. Then you will call upon me and come and pray to me, and I will listen to you. You will seek me and find me when you seek me with all your heart. I will be found by you," declares the LORD, "and will bring you back from captivity. I will gather you from all the nations and places where I have banished you," declares the LORD, "and will bring you back to the place from which I carried you into exile."
(Jeremiah 29:11-14)

For it is by grace you have been saved, through faith-and this not from yourselves, it is the gift of God- not by works, so that no one can boast. For we are God's workmanship, created in Christ Jesus to do good works, which God prepared in advance for us to do.
(Ephesians 2:8-10)

It is my hope that you have meditated on the Scriptures above, and have sought diligently for God's Wisdom and understanding.

A Living Sacrifice: Chapter Eight

This chapter in no way, is about God's divine selection or predestination; however, with passages of Scripture such as the ones you've just read, one could certainly make a case for predestination, and the Sovereignty of God, verses man's very limited free will. My intent however, is not necessarily to show that we are predestined by God and specifically chosen by God, as God rejects others; however, for the sake of argument, I do believe that God has a specific purpose in choosing those who would become His children, and that we are chosen from the creation and the foundation of the world. If we get anything at all out of the Scriptures, just read, let it be this: God is our Creator, God is sovereign over His creation, and God alone is in control! And so having said that, when we seek God's will for our lives, outside of His divine purpose, which has already been predestined, then we take control away from God and put it into our own hands.

Even when we seek to do good works and to bring glory to God, we can be just as much in sin as if we were living our lives in utter idleness. The good works that God has purposed in each individual life, the endowment of spiritual gifts, the talent, skill, or ability to excel in certain areas, the grace and amount of faith given by God to accomplish whatever He has ordained and purposed in our lives, can only be accomplished in Him, and in Him alone. Unfortunately, this is not how many in the church today live out their faith. Many believers say that they believe in, and trust in the sovereignty of God, that He is in control, but yet live as though somehow God saved us to will and to act, to help us accomplish our own wills, as we pursue happiness and the things we covet. A job, a house, financial independence, or whatever it may be. We think God's will is somehow intertwined with our humanity according to our own human perspective, rather than understanding God's will to be spiritual and predestined, and accomplished only through His divine intervention, for His glory, and for His glory alone!

A Living Sacrifice: Chapter Eight

Now if God knew us before we were born, if He knitted us together in our mother's womb, if His eyes saw our unformed bodies as we were woven together in the depths of the earth, and He was preparing us for His purpose as He tells Jeremiah, then why do many Christians in the twenty first century, act as if they doubt or question who it is we belong to, or who's will we ought to be surrendered to?

We are not our own, remember? We have all been bought and paid for by the precious blood of Jesus. What about God's plans for us do we not get? Do we truly understand that we have been created in Christ Jesus for a purpose, and that purpose is to do the work that God has predestined for us to do? Do we believe God's Word to be simply only general revelation, or is it alive? I believe the Word of God to be alive and active, powerfully and specifically speaking to every detail of our lives. Whether or not we live our lives according to God's Word and His perfect will, which He has purposed in each one of our lives, will depend upon our obedience to lose our lives, and surrender all. Once again, in Matthew 16:24-26, Jesus says this: ***Then Jesus said to his disciples, "If anyone would come after me, he must deny himself and take up his cross and follow me. For whoever wants to save his life will lose it, but whoever loses his life for me will find it. What good will it be for a man if he gains the whole world, yet forfeits his soul?"***

Are we to believe the above passage of Scripture is speaking solely about our salvation? What about after we come to Jesus, once we have been born again? Do we not have to continually take up our cross, follow Jesus, and lose our lives? I say yes, and brokenness and abiding in Jesus, and seeking to be filled with the grace of God, is exactly what this entire book is about. And as burdensome as this is, it is worth repeating, that many Christians in the church today have no spiritual understanding what it means to abide in Jesus, or lose their lives for Christ's sake, and thus have yet to experience the spiritual.

A Living Sacrifice: Chapter Eight

Many churches today, in congregations across America, have become nothing more than mere social clubs, where its members just happen to share the same beliefs. Why? Is it because God has left His church? Absolutely not! God is sovereign, He alone is in control, and He will never leave us nor forsake us; however, there are millions of believers that leave God every day. They might praise him with their lips but yet their hearts are far from Him, and they never even learn to walk with Him and trust in Him completely by surrendering their lives to His control. As many live out their faith, many come to Jesus and yet remain in control of everything they do, they never learn to fully let go, nor begin to understand it is the Holy Spirit's power, that will accomplish and provide everything they will need for this life; that is in Christ Jesus! Just look around at the church today, look within your own congregation, if in fact, you even attend church. Do you see the compromise, the carnality and the lack of spiritual attitudes within the church? I certainly do, and I am burdened and overwhelmed with grief for the church. However, God is sovereign and He alone is still in control; therefore, I never lose heart, because I am constantly reminded, that Jesus has given us His promises, and has given us His very Spirit, to fulfill them.

But why then, with such awesome promises, do we continue to forsake Him? Why do we continue to seek His will and yet cling to the world? Why are our relationships with our brothers and sisters in Christ simply social and non-transparent? Why is our worship unto the Lord, simply an obligation or a discipline? Why do we continue to be busy bodies for Jesus, as we then boast about the works that we do? Because, we are living out the faith in the flesh, and not in the Spirit! I believe our greatest mistake, is to intertwine our human experience with the spiritual.

A Living Sacrifice: Chapter Eight

    We are not here to simply experience our humanity, we are here to partake in the spiritual, to participate in the divine nature, as we experience this abundant life Jesus gives, as we now have the Kingdom of God within. We see this in 2Peter 1:3-4:

    His divine power has given us everything we need for life and godliness through our knowledge of him who called us by his own glory and goodness. Through these he has given us his very great and precious promises, so that through them you may participate in the divine nature and escape the corruption in the world caused by evil desires. Does this abundant life, include the blessings of living our human lives here on earth with peace, joy, and even happiness? Absolutely! But our problem is that many in the church today are focused on their humanity, and being happy, as they deny the spiritual. In other words, we focus only on what we can see, as we walk by sight and not by faith. God has come to turn our lives right side up, and even though having received salvation through a faith in Jesus Christ, many remain in the futility of their humanity, never learning to surrender, continuing to live upside down, clinging still to the world, and their human experience.

    Is it the will of God, for the Church to save the world? To rid the world of poverty, suffering, and all evil? Humanism suggests that we are left to our own devices to solve the world's problems, and although in this life, we as the body of Christ, are called to love, to have compassion, to care for the poor and for the orphan and widow, we can no more save the world we live in, then we could have saved ourselves. The Scriptures tell us that we have been delivered from this present evil age, thus for us it is spiritual, and we are not here to solve the world's problems, because the problem of evil, begins in the hearts of sinful man, and only God can change the heart!

    Jesus saved the world by saving us, and all those who would come to the truth. Thus, we are called to trust in God, and in the sufficiency of Christ's sacrifice, to have accomplished this work.

A Living Sacrifice: Chapter Eight

These are the words of Jesus Himself. In John 4:34, Jesus says: ***"My food," said Jesus, "is to do the will of him who sent me and to finish his work."*** Also, in John 19:30 Jesus speaks from the cross:
When he had received the drink, Jesus said, "It is finished." With that, he bowed his head and gave up his spirit.

And so if Jesus has finished the work His Father has sent Him to finish, why do Christians somehow believe we are left here on earth to deal with evil, and continue the work that Jesus Christ has already finished? Evil is a result of human hearts filled with deceitfulness, and flows forth not only from humans, but other created beings, for Satan himself, was once an exalted angelic being, created by God, and who was cast down from heaven by God from his position of great dignity and honor, cast down to earth, with all the fallen angels, his demons, where he continues to this day to work his evil and maintain his evil influence upon the earth. Evil will exist as long as Satan and humans continue to exist, because evil begins and continues in the heart of man. Though evil has been dealt with, and defeated at the cross where our Lord laid down His life, as long as human beings continue to reject Jesus Christ, evil will continue to not only exist through Satan's influence and through sinful man, but will continue to flourish. And as the Scriptures teach, I believe evil will increase in the last days and become more rampant, just as Jesus says in Matthew 24:12-13: ***Because of the increase of wickedness, the love of most will grow cold, but he who stands firm to the end will be saved.***

We must remember, that evil has been around since Adam fell in the Garden. Why am I saying all of this? Because I believe, many Christians think that solving the world's problems, is the will of God for the church, and I would disagree. To believe that the will of God for the church is to rid the world of poverty, suffering, and all evil, is a human idea, not a Biblical one. Evil is the result of a fallen world and sin, and dealing with sin is the work of God.

A Living Sacrifice: Chapter Eight

God has dealt with evil, for God sent His only begotten Son, that we might be delivered from evil. Now I am not suggesting that we are not to continue on with Christ's ministry, as we live out our lives in the Spirit, because as we know, those who have the Spirit of Christ indwelling them, that the fruit of the Spirit is love. Therefore, as a result, we love and press on with the ministry of Christ because His Spirit compels us. We are called to be the Light and Salt of the earth, as we care for the sick, for those that suffer, for the children, for the widows, for the poor, for the prisoners, and for all who are lost, and it is because we have Christ in us, that God's love compels us to shine in a dark world, and to love our neighbor as ourselves.

And though this might momentarily impact a dark world, it can never change the world, or rid the world of evil, it is a love that compels us, so that God might be glorified, and that hearts might be changed as Christ and Christ crucified is preached to the lost, both with our lips and through our actions. Every good work is predestined and ordained by God for one purpose, and that is that the gospel of Jesus Christ might be preached, and that man would turn their hearts toward God. Therefore, we must examine our hearts, and ask ourselves, has our faith cultivated a relationship with God, or is our experience nothing more than humanism, as we live according to a human religious philosophy, as we read in 2Timothy 3:5a, **_having a form of godliness but denying its power._**

I can almost guarantee you, that if I were to ask many Christians in the Church, what they believe God's will is, and how it is lived out and accomplished in their lives, I would get many different answers. I suggest, for the most part, I would get many practical examples, as the spiritual is ignored. I believe many in the Church are unable to express their understanding of the spiritual, especially the youth, because many are simply not being discipled and lead to the Spirit, and thus have not been imparted with spiritual attitudes.

A Living Sacrifice: Chapter Eight

Having a spiritual attitude or spiritual fervor is foreign to many Christians, and unfortunately the Christians that do trust in the power of the Holy Spirit, having a spiritual attitude and an eternal perspective, are by many, looked upon and labeled, as I have already stated, either too charismatic, spiritually prideful, or just dismissed as randomly strange. I believe the Scriptures are clear, but do we all truly see the Scriptures as truth, or in our carnal minds, simply another ideology or world view, up for interpretation? Now I realize there are disputable matters in the Scriptures, but the Word of God in no way is an ideology. Which brings me to the idea, that some in the church might believe that to defend a Christian world view against the ideologies and views of the world, is somehow God's will for the church. Of course, we absolutely are commanded to take to the public square, and infiltrate it with the gospel of Jesus Christ, it is for this very reason, that God has entrusted us with, **"the good news,"** His message of reconciliation; however, this is accomplished only through God's direction as we are carried along by the Holy Spirit.

Remember what Paul told young Timothy? ***The LORD did not give us a spirit of fear, but of power, and of love, and of a sound mind.*** You see, it is the Spirit that gives us this sound mind, that gives us understanding into the gospel and the Word of God, it is the Spirit that gives us the power, the resolve, and the boldness to take this truth to the world. But to believe our faith in Christ is simply another world view, ideology, or simply another belief, is in my opinion conforming to the world, by putting an unspiritual label on God's Truth. Christianity is true, it is not a world view, nor is it an ideology, it is ***Truth***! We have received this truth through a faith in Jesus Christ, and for us who believe, it has transformed us spiritually, ushered us into the Kingdom of God, and has brought us into a relationship with our Creator.

A Living Sacrifice: Chapter Eight

It is futile to argue against world views or ideologies with those in the world. For the very reason that secularism, scientism, naturalism, postmodernism, and moral relativism exist, just to name a few of the philosophies of man, is because of the evil within man's heart, and Satan's attack on God's truth. I believe that when we look upon God's truth from a human perspective and treat it as simply another worldview or ideology, we can get caught up to believe it is somehow our calling to change the world with our own passionate ideas, outside of the very oracles of God. However, when human arguments cause us to reflect upon our own intellectual ideas, rather than on Christ, this can be dangerous. Anyone who proclaims the name of Jesus Christ, ought to lead others in one direction, and that is to Christ, to His cross, and to His Spirit. Just as we see in America, even if the church could change our society or culture, (which it has), and even if our society or culture were to be governed by God's Word, (which to an extent it is), sin would still reign in man's heart, and thus because evil abounds, in reality, our culture remains unchanged. You see, Jesus did not come to change our world, but to change us and all who are in the world, spiritually. It is those that believe in Jesus, who are taken out of this world spiritually, to live eternally in His Kingdom now and forever. We are not of this world, we are but pilgrims on our way to our homeland, and we are not here to bring peace or morality to the world, but to bring the gospel which changes the hearts of men and thus bringing peace between men and their Creator, Almighty God! Jesus Himself says that He did not come to bring peace, but to divide.
Luke 12:49-51: **"I have come to bring fire on the earth, and how I wish it were already kindled! But I have a baptism to undergo, and how distressed I am until it is completed! Do you think I came to bring peace on earth? No, I tell you, but division."**

A Living Sacrifice: Chapter Eight

Spiritual wisdom and knowledge into the moral and sovereign will of God is not revealed to those in the world, it is only revealed to His church, for only those in the body of Christ have understanding. His Word is to be preached to His church, and not to the world, except of course, His message of reconciliation, the gospel of Jesus Christ. To believe that preaching the gospel to the world, and preaching to the unspiritual world a world view or an ideology are the same, is ignorant. Preaching the gospel is trusting in the power of God, as man is lead by His Spirit, but treating God's truth as a world view or ideology, is denying the power of God, as man tries to change a culture, with truth yes, but which leaves the hearts of men unchanged. Romans 1:16 says this: ***I am not ashamed of the gospel, because it is the power of God for the salvation of everyone who believes: first for the Jew, then for the Gentile.***

God has commanded us to be concerned with saving souls as we live out our lives in obedience to His moral and sovereign will. We are not here to change the world from an intellectual, political, social, or even a moral perspective; we are here only to reach others with the gospel of Jesus Christ. As believers we are called to imitate Jesus, and are commanded to live holy lives and to love our neighbor, and this can only be accomplished by His Spirit. We cannot simply indoctrinate others with the Lord's commandments and with His truth, and compel them to obey God, as we live out our Christian lives. Only Christ Jesus Himself can change our hearts. It is through the gospel we are changed, for it is the power of God, and it is by faith, for the Bible teaches that faith comes by hearing and hearing by the Word of God, and this is accomplished in our hearts, for it is with our hearts we believe. When the world chooses to believe and abide in Christ, that is when the world will be changed, one heart at a time. All that we do, if in fact, we are being directed and governed by the Holy Spirit, is for one purpose, and that is to bring the world to Christ, all for His glory!

A Living Sacrifice: Chapter Eight

This is why Jesus Christ Himself came, to fulfill the Scriptures, to lay down His life for the redemption of mankind for the forgiveness of sins, and to bring the Father's children unto Himself, through His Truth! In John 18:36-37: *Jesus said, "My kingdom is not of this world. If it were, my servants would fight to prevent my arrest by the Jews. But now my kingdom is from another place." "You are a king, then!" said Pilate. Jesus answered, "You are right in saying I am a king. In fact, for this reason I was born, and for this I came into the world, to testify to the truth. Everyone on the side of truth listens to me."*

This is the will of God, to take forth the gospel of Jesus Christ, and to be a witness to His truth. When we are filled with the Holy Spirit, we will be governed by the Holy Spirit, and then, and only then, will every good work be accomplished through us, to lead others to Christ and thus bring glory to God! We are given this command in Matthew 28:18-20: *Then Jesus came to them and said, "All authority in heaven and on earth has been given to me. Therefore go and make disciples of all nations, baptizing them in the name of the Father and of the Son and of the Holy Spirit, and teaching them to obey everything I have commanded you. And surely I am with you always, to the very end of the age."*
And again, in 1 John 2:15-17, it says:

Do not love the world or anything in the world. If anyone loves the world, the love of the Father is not in him. For everything in the world-the cravings of sinful man, the lust of his eyes and the boasting of what he has and does-comes not from the Father but from the world. The world and its desires pass away, but the man who does the will of God lives forever.

Now of course I have already expounded upon the above passage of Scripture in Chapter six, but what I want to take note of here, is its final exhortation. *"The world and its desires pass away, but the man who does the will of God lives forever."*

A Living Sacrifice: Chapter Eight

It is obvious that the world and the desires of man in his flesh are contrary to doing the will of God, but to take it one step even further, if we as believers are to live out our lives in the will of God, we must then look to His divine power, and not to ourselves or to the world.

The one *who is in you, is greater than the one who is in the world*, 1 John 4:4-6: **You, dear children, are from God and have overcome them, because the one who is in you is greater than the one who is in the world. They are from the world and therefore speak from the viewpoint of the world, and the world listens to them. We are from God, and whoever knows God listens to us; but whoever is not from God does not listen to us. This is how we recognize the Spirit of truth and the spirit of falsehood.**

My point once again, is that the will of God is accomplished in the power of the Holy Spirit. If we are followers of Christ, we must seek to be filled with the Spirit of Christ, whom now indwells us, if we are to live according to His good, pleasing and perfect will.

The Scriptures are filled with revelation from God, and it has not been my intent in this chapter to go over the many specific commandments of God, revealing His specific will. My intent has been to help bring understanding into the spiritual, and to place emphasis on the Spirit, and on the spiritual attitude we must have in approaching God and His Word, where, *"Then You Will Be Able to Test and Approve What God's Will Is."*

As we continue discussing the will of God in chapter nine, my hope is that you might have a better understanding into the sovereignty of God, His very purpose for the church, and why we exist in Christ Jesus.

CHAPTER NINE:

His Good, Pleasing and Perfect Will........ (The Sovereignty of God)

Can we know why we exist? I mean can we truly understand and do we believe, that we exist for a purpose, and this purpose involves a plan that God Himself has predestined? Now maybe we are unable to completely wrap our finite minds around this, but yes, God has given us a glimpse into eternity and into His sovereignty, and thus we have been given limited understanding into His plan, as it is being accomplished according to His good, pleasing and perfect will. Do you truly believe that you are "in Christ," for a purpose, to be used as an intricate part of His plan? It is my hope that now you do, and that the Spirit has brought you enlightenment and a greater understanding. I believe that it was not only to save us, or give us eternal life, but that God has shown us mercy and has given us this gift of grace for a greater purpose.

A Living Sacrifice: Chapter Nine

Now we of course, have not been given full revelation into God's sovereign plan, to the extent that we have knowledge into every intricate detail, and this is why I believe that predestination and election are two separate doctrines. Predestination must still succeed under the agency of man's free will, and is still at work within human history, whereas election was solely accomplished under the intervening hand of God, and has already taken place within salvation history past. It is not my intent to discuss these doctrines; however, I mention them because it is important to know that we are servants of God, and He has called us into this life as a bond-servant, that is only accomplished and lived out in the power of His Spirit yes, but is also dependent upon our obedience. I have discussed the resounding theme of this book throughout every chapter, that we mature by the surrendering of our lives to Christ, as we are filled with the power of His Spirit. I have discussed also the will of God and the only way by which His will is accomplished within the church and within our individual lives. Now we will see that it is only the will of God, His sovereign plan to accomplish His will through the church, that is good, pleasing and perfect.

It is not our human understanding or interpretation, and nor is it clinging to the world and the world views, the philosophies of this age, or the psychology of the mind that will determine how we accomplish the good, pleasing, and perfect will of God. It is God and God alone who will accomplish His good, pleasing, and perfect will, and if we want to be a part of it, we must learn to die to self, offer our bodies as living sacrifices, take up our cross, and understand that only by His Spirit filling our empty human vessel can this happen.

A Living Sacrifice: Chapter Nine

We cannot determine the will of God simply by our every day living, especially when the world is pulling us to and fro and in every direction. We must learn to separate the spiritual from the practical. The spiritual may be played out in practical ways in our every day living, but what is empowered by the Holy Spirit in accordance with the good, pleasing, and perfect will of God, can only be accomplished spiritually. In other words, we cannot look to simply the tangible or practical, we must allow the Spirit to help us walk by faith and not by sight, looking to Jesus, in all that we do.

We must learn to let go and not trust in our human ability to accomplish God's will. Will God use and enable our abilities to accomplish His will here on earth? Absolutely! It is God who has gifted us with our abilities for His purpose; however, we must learn to seek understanding of the spiritual, where the Spirit operates. As children of God we are either doing His will, or we are not. Abiding in Christ and living in accordance to His commandments is God's will for us, and having learned to walk in the light and having understood the victory over the power of sin in our lives, this is a good, pleasing and perfect place to be; however, what good works are we accomplishing for the Kingdom of God, and how is God using us, both as the body, and individually?

We must learn; therefore, that we are transformed through the renewing of our minds, and it is in our surrendering where we begin to walk in this spiritual attitude sustained by the power of His Spirit. Many have created this false sense, that the only difference between the church and the world is that we simply hold the answers concerning truth. Many in the church today are so shallow and carnal, some think our salvation, and who we are in Christ, is about nothing more than living happy lives, as we point our finger at an immoral world.

A Living Sacrifice: Chapter Nine

Many in the church, look at the world just as the world does, from a human perspective, and feel that somehow we can point our fingers at the world arrogantly, as we hold the key to all truth. And though it is spiritual, and darkness hates the light, this attitude, only further fuels hate, and is one reason why those in the church are looked upon by the world as hypocrites, in line with Satan's plan. Of course, the church has been given knowledge into all truth, because truth has been revealed to us by the authority of the Scriptures, which we also know to be the perfect and inerrant Word of God; however, the church is not called to look at the world by worldly standards, nor are we called to change the world, with our own righteous indignation.

Christ has died for the world, but for those who believe, those in Christ, are we truly learning to abide in Christ, as we live out our surrendered lives, walking in the power of the Holy Spirit? Have we truly left the things of the world behind to press on toward spiritual maturity? If God is real, and our faith in God real, then where are the spiritually mature in Christ? What is empowering the church today? Is it our effort, our ingenuity, our strength, our righteousness, our idolatry, our rituals and traditions? What? Can we truly say that it is the Spirit of God, His power, moving the church today in the twenty first century? Now God is Sovereign and His will is being accomplished; in fact, His Kingdom is eternal, and all has been predestined. Before the foundation of the world His plan was formed, executed, and finished. Once again, you heard me right! Christ Himself uttered it from the cross two thousand years ago, as I use the greek word for emphasis, "***Tetelasti!***" It is finished! Our problem as believers is that we try intellectually to wrap our finite minds around the spiritual, the eternal, and the power of God, as we deny the Spirit that transforms us, and imparts us with understanding into all three.

A Living Sacrifice: Chapter Nine

Although we press on with our very best effort, and though having our hearts in the right place, we deny the very God we profess. Although clinging to the truth with all our might, we are spiritually bankrupt wondering how we got to this place where the love of many has grown cold, and how we've arrived at a time where many have left the teaching of sound doctrine to listen to what their itching ears want to hear, and all the while, as we ignore and allow such subtle complacency and carnality to creep into the church in America! And thus we are warned to be ready, for Jesus will come like a thief in the night, swiftly and without warning! Our God will not be mocked, for He is not dead, He is alive, and He never slumbers.

When I speak to believers, those who profess to be believers, especially when I am not a pastor, but one who simply sits humbly in the pews, and as I express this view of the carnal Church, filled with weak minded Christians, many in the church refuse to judge or admit, and or agree. But, the reason many are weak minded, is because many have received intellectually the things of God, which has only gone to further encourage them to depend on themselves, and rely upon their carnal minds, rather than have been discipled, to depend upon the Spirit and upon God's power. It is carnal and unspiritual to think that the Church can survive on human intellect. We are *new creations,* we have been transformed from the flesh to the spirit, and our lives are now hidden with Christ in God. The Holy Spirit is our teacher, and we do not need to be appeased with simple intellectual and practical teachings; we need the Word of God to now instruct us, in the power of the Spirit, to live out our purposed lives, in Christ! We are simply not being lead to the *cross,* or being *discipled* to trust in the power of God and in the filling of the Holy Spirit, and thus we are not being the disciples of Jesus, He has called us to be.

A Living Sacrifice: Chapter Nine

Is the mystery of Christ and His gospel, revealed to the first century church, different than the mystery that has been revealed to you and I? Is it because we live in a different age or culture, that our faith is simply played out differently than in the first century? No, It is because of carnality, trusting in God yes, but denying His power. We liken the Word of God, to some practical life application, as we interpret the Scriptures from a human perspective, rather than understanding, that the Scriptures are active and alive, and are meant to transform us with the wisdom of God, by the power of His Spirit!

And, with such carnal attitudes, we walk out of church so proud that we have somehow kept our promises to God by fulfilling our weekly obligation, when in eternity we have not grown, not one inch nearer to God. We can not know the good, pleasing, and perfect will of God, nor understand His sovereignty in such a condition; in fact, it is as foreign to us as to those in the world when our inner man is so void and emptied of the Holy Spirit of God. Only by His Spirit have we been transformed into a *new creature*, now enabled to submit and surrender to Him. Only by His Spirit are we now enabled to do anything for the glory of God. To give you a practical illustration, I see carnality in many in the church. They claim to love the LORD, and they know His Word, because they read His Word, and have been trained up in the ways they should go, and though we can never know what is going on in their hearts, unless they actually somehow reveal it, we can also never presume to know their own personal relationship with God. However, I can tell you from personal experience, that there are many in the church that do not seem to outwardly discuss or express their love for the LORD, and although God's Word, may not be far from their hearts, it certainly at times can be far from their lips. Many are unspiritual and carnal.

A Living Sacrifice: Chapter Nine

Now, I am not saying that anyone in this condition is unsaved, but when we look at such carnality, what I believe is holding them back from worshipping the LORD in spirit and in truth, is an unsurrendered life, still under the influence of the flesh. And in the church, regardless of the age of anyone within the body of Christ, it is filled with young innocent babes that have no clue what it means to surrender to the Spirit, and grow up in Christ! Paul addresses this very issue in his first letter to the Corinthians, which was not placed within God's breathed Word simply to give you and I a look see into the history of the church at Corinth, but to warn us concerning this issue which has no doubt been within the body of Christ throughout church history, and continues to this very day.

Brothers, I could not address you as spiritual but as worldly- mere infants in Christ. I gave you milk, not solid food, for you were not yet ready for it. Indeed, you are still not ready. You are still worldly. For since there is jealousy and quarreling among you, are you not worldly? Are you not acting like mere men? For when one says, "I follow Paul," and another, "I follow Apollos," are you not mere men? (1Corinthians 3:1-4)

Now as we can see in the above passage, Paul is rebuking the church at Corinth, and calling them carnal for more than one reason, and he specifically mentions jealousy and quarreling. We can also look to James 4:1-10, as the Lord addresses this same carnal behavior among believers, and gives us understanding as to why it occurs.

A Living Sacrifice: Chapter Nine

What causes fights and quarrels among you? Don't they come from your desires that battle within you? You want something but don't get it. You kill and covet, but you cannot have what you want. You quarrel and fight. You do not have, because you do not ask God. When you ask, you do not receive, because you ask with wrong motives, that you may spend what you get on your pleasures. You adulterous people, don't you know that friendship with the world is hatred toward God? Anyone who chooses to be a friend of the world becomes an enemy of God.

Or do you think Scripture says without reason that the Spirit he caused to live in us envies intensely? But he gives us more grace. That is why Scripture says: "God opposes the proud but gives grace to the humble." Submit yourselves, then, to God. Resist the devil, and he will flee from you. Come near to God and he will come near to you. Wash your hands, you sinners, and purify your hearts, you double-minded. Grieve, mourn and wail. Change your laughter to mourning and your joy to gloom. Humble yourselves before the Lord, and he will lift you up.

The same carnality that Paul addresses in the church at Corinth, and the understanding we receive in the above passage in James, is exactly on point. Carnality is leaving the Spirit. Galatians 3:3 says: ***Are you so foolish? Having begun in the Spirit, you are now being made perfect by the flesh?*** It is not only a turning away from relying upon the Scriptures of God and the spiritual truths revealed there in, but it is a turning away from the Holy Spirit Himself, and thus turning back once again to the things of the world. The carnal church and the carnal believer moves in much the same way. Many remain in the world and in their futile thinking, as they rely upon the flesh, never learning or willing to submit and surrender completely to the Spirit.

A Living Sacrifice: Chapter Nine

All God really requires of us, is surrender. God wants to give us a a broken spirit, and a contrite heart. For it is for His purpose and for His glory that we were created, to do His good, pleasing and perfect will. So, how do we know His good, pleasing and perfect will? And how do we understand our responsibility to do His will in these bodies of flesh, and yet reconcile that with an Almighty Sovereign God? That my friend is a very good question, so let us once again, go back to the beginning, shall we?

> ***So God created man in his own image, in the image of God he created him; male and female he created them.***
> (Genesis 1:27)

We know that we have all sinned and fallen short of the glory of God, and that we live upon a fallen earth where Satan is the prince and the power of the air, directing all evil and destruction in his path, roaming the earth to and fro, seeking whom he might devour. Like puppets with free will, the devil pulls upon the strings of our deceitful heart and tugs upon the strings of our sinful nature, to lead us into darkness and to keep us from the light. However, this is not how we were created. We were all created in the very image of God, to walk along side our Creator in sweet fellowship. Before the fall, Adam was spiritually perfect, and this is what God has intended for His children, to bring us back into that very same sweet fellowship, to fill us with His Spirit, that we might bare fruit as we walk in His divine power.

Now of course, though our position with God has been restored, our condition will not be made perfect, until we physically enter into the Kingdom of God; however, spiritually, the Scriptures tell us, that Christ has delivered us from this present evil age, and as it says in Ephesians 2:14-18, Christ is our peace, and He has destroyed the dividing wall of hostility between God and us all.

A Living Sacrifice: Chapter Nine

For he himself is our peace, who has made the two one and has destroyed the barrier, the dividing wall of hostility, by abolishing in his flesh the law with its commandments and regulations. His purpose was to create in himself one new man out of the two, thus making peace, and in this one body to reconcile both of them to God through the cross, by which he put to death their hostility. He came and preached peace to you who were far away and peace to those who were near. For through him we both have access to the Father by one Spirit.

This does not mean that there is no longer the battle between the flesh and the spirit; however, it does give us insight into how our fellowship now with the Father has been restored and how His Holy Spirit has accomplished this for all believers. And this is how His will, His good, pleasing and perfect will is accomplished. God has chosen to reveal Himself to sinful man, and by using man whom has been reconciled, redeemed and justified through His mercy and by His grace, empowered by His Spirit, His sovereign will is accomplished.

Praise be to the God and Father of our Lord Jesus Christ, who has blessed us in the heavenly realms with every spiritual blessing in Christ.
(Ephesians 1:3)

How then do we know God's will, His good, pleasing, and perfect will? We can not know what has not been revealed, but we can know what God has already revealed. In Ephesians 5:8-10 it says this: *For you were once darkness, but now you are light in the Lord. Live as children of light (for the fruit of the light consists in all goodness, righteousness and truth) and find out what pleases the Lord. Have nothing to do with the fruitless deeds of darkness, but rather expose them.*

A Living Sacrifice: Chapter Nine

Are we to find out what pleases the LORD through osmosis? Are we to search for it like buried treasure? Are we to embark upon a great journey searching for it? Or has the wisdom of God already been revealed? This is what God's Word says:

The LORD is exalted, for he dwells on high; he will fill Zion with justice and righteousness. He will be the sure foundation for your times, a rich store of salvation and wisdom and knowledge; the fear of the LORD is the key to this treasure.
(Isaiah 33:5-6)

His divine power has given us everything we need for life and godliness through our knowledge of him who called us by his own glory and goodness. Through these he has given us his very great and precious promises, so that through them you may participate in the divine nature and escape the corruption in the world caused by evil desires.
(2 Peter 1:3-4)

My purpose is that they may be encouraged in heart and united in love, so that they may have the full riches of complete understanding, in order that they may know the mystery of God, namely, Christ, in whom are hidden all the treasures of wisdom and knowledge.
(Colossians 2:2-13)

We hold the key to God's wisdom and knowledge, and it is to fear Him! Through Christ, we have everything we need through His divine power, as we participate in the very nature of God, and this mystery of God, has been revealed through Christ in whom are hidden all the treasures of wisdom and knowledge.

A Living Sacrifice: Chapter Nine

But I know, I already know what people would say, people are looking for knowledge to be just a little bit more practical, something we can actually grasp and fathom and wrap our finite minds around. But I say, that is exactly where we fall short. And with this carnal attitude, our hope in Christ becomes then, about us, and interpreting the things of God only in the tangible as if it is somehow of human origin. Our faith then becomes rooted in our own intelligence and thus, in what makes sense according only to our unspiritual human perspective, as our religion then seeks to be comfortable within our own reality; which then, in our hearts and minds, makes it just that, simply another religion.

But I implore you to come out of your comfort zone, where you are living according to the flesh, and come now into the unknown, where Jesus is, and live now in the spirit. This is where the broken in spirit and contrite in heart live in the power of the Holy Spirit!

We are children of God and His Kingdom is within, we are in His kingdom now! Jesus is waiting, His Spirit wants to fill you with the treasures of His wisdom and knowledge, reveal your spiritual gifts, and then take you and use your vessel for His glory to do exceedingly more than you could ever ask or imagine, to do the unthinkable, to accomplish the good, pleasing and perfect will of God.

For we are God's workmanship created in Christ Jesus to do good works, which God has prepared in advance for us to do.
(Ephesians 2:10)

A Living Sacrifice: Chapter Nine

<u>Behold! The Sovereignty of God</u>:

But now, this is what the LORD says--he who created you, O Jacob, he who formed you, O Israel: "Fear not, for I have redeemed you; I have summoned you by name; you are mine. When you pass through the waters, I will be with you; and when you pass through the rivers, they will not sweep over you. When you walk through the fire, you will not be burned; the flames will not set you ablaze. For I am the LORD, your God, the Holy One of Israel, your Savior; I give Egypt for your ransom, Cush and Seba in your stead. Since you are precious and honored in my sight, and because I love you, I will give men in exchange for you, and people in exchange for your life. Do not be afraid, for I am with you; I will bring your children from the east and gather you from the west. I will say to the north, 'Give them up!' and to the south, 'Do not hold them back.' Bring my sons from afar and my daughters from the ends of the earth-- everyone who is called by my name, whom I created for my glory, whom I formed and made." Lead out those who have eyes but are blind, who have ears but are deaf. All the nations gather together and the peoples assemble. Which of them foretold this and proclaimed to us the former things? Let them bring in their witnesses to prove they were right, so that others may hear and say, "It is true." "You are my witnesses," declares the LORD," and my servant whom I have chosen, so that you may know and believe me and understand that I am he. Before me no god was formed, nor will there be one after me. I, even I, am the LORD, and apart from me there is no savior."

(Isaiah 43:1-11)

A Living Sacrifice: Chapter Nine

    This is God, whom has brought you out of darkness and into His marvelous light! This is the LORD your God who formed you in your mother's womb, and who knew you and created you from the foundation of the world, and this is the LORD your God who says: "Come, all you who are heavy laden and burdened, take My yoke, for My burden is light and My yoke is easy, come to Me, find rest and be saved." But do not think, it is without cost, for I say unto you that you must lay down your life, die daily and take up your cross. My promises are true, and I will never leave you nor forsake you, and upon believing you will receive the promised Holy Spirit as a deposit guaranteeing your inheritance, for you have been made heirs, co-heirs with Christ, and you have entered into My Kingdom. All I ask is that you become like Me, the greatest servant of them all, go out unto all the earth and make disciples of all nations, baptizing them in the name of the Father, the Son, and the Holy Spirit. But remember, you must abide in Me always, there you will bare much fruit, but apart from Me you can do nothing.

    What then is our responsibility? It is obedience! And apart from Christ we can do nothing, but through Him we can accomplish all things. We must surrender the flesh, stop thinking on our terms, stop acting upon our own ideas on how God works, and stop believing that our Christian liberty and freedom means that we can do things as free thinkers. We are to be lead by the Holy Spirit, He will give us direction and guidance! Our very freedom in Christ, has been poured out upon us, to redeem us from the bondage and from the power of sin, and from the yoke of the Law. The purpose of this new found freedom in Christ, is to lead us more and more nearer to the cross, where by we are called to then surrender our very freedom, to live now as a bond servant of Christ, in bondage to His will and to His righteousness. So yes we have freedom, but it is to be exercised in the Spirit, to live now for the will of God, all to His glory.

A Living Sacrifice: Chapter Nine

This is where the sovereignty of God and our responsibility meets, and we are simply responsible to live in obedience to the Holy Spirit in the things that have been revealed, and also the things yet to be revealed. God's will is good, it is pleasing and it is perfect, and God is sovereign! We are called to surrender all, and be filled with the Spirit, that we would walk in the Spirit, and that with our minds now on the things of the Spirit, we will desire the things of the Spirit, that we might now act out in love, manifesting the fruit of the Spirit. And as the Spirit cultivates our gifts, He will use us according to the amount of faith God has given to each one, to accomplish God's purpose, and the works He has prepared in advance for us to walk in.

God's Sovereignty simply means, He is God, He alone is in control, and it is His will, that will be accomplished! In fact, as I have already stated, His will is eternal and has been accomplished, and it has and will be and is, with or without us. But lest we forget, that God has loved us, and in His mercy has chosen to use each one of us. And I don't know about you, but I want to be apart of God's sovereign plan, *"His good, pleasing and perfect will."* I want to be used by Him, that my life would be a living sacrifice that has brought glory, honor, and praise to my God, my LORD and my Savior. Yes, I want to hear the words, well done my good and faithful servant, but as those words resonate in my heart, I know it is not about me, but about Christ glorified, and what His mercy has done and how His grace and power has accomplished His will through a sinner like myself. It is about God Almighty, the Holy One of Israel, the King of kings, and LORD of lords, for He alone is worthy, and all glory is His.

CHAPTER TEN:

A Conclusion of The Matter........

Now all has been heard; here is the conclusion of the matter: Fear God and keep his commandments, for this is the whole [duty] of man. For God will bring every deed into judgment, including every hidden thing, whether it is good or evil.
(Ecclesiastes 12:13-14)

Solomon, as we know from the Scriptures, was a very wise and wealthy king; in fact, we know that as he prayed to the LORD for wisdom, he was blessed by the LORD with wisdom, and eventually given great wealth and power. However, In all his wealth and power, it was ultimately the wisdom of God that stood the test, and as Solomon himself acknowledged, that although we are to live here on earth, it is all meaningless without God. For nothing but God, can bring man true contentment and satisfaction, not work, not money, not possessions, not life itself. For without God, everything under the sun is futile and meaningless, but with God, everything under the Son, is then quite the opposite, it is good, pleasing, and perfect, as we walk in Him, and in His perfect will.

A Living Sacrifice: Chapter Ten

Therefore, since Christ suffered in his body, arm yourselves also with the same attitude, because he who has suffered in his body is done with sin. As a result, he does not live the rest of his earthly life for evil human desires, but rather for the will of Go.
(1Peter 4:1-2)

Slaves, obey your earthly masters with respect and fear, and with sincerity of heart, just as you would obey Christ. Obey them not only to win their favor when their eye is on you, but like slaves of Christ, doing the will of God from your heart. Serve wholeheartedly, as if you were serving the Lord, not men, because you know that the Lord will reward everyone for whatever good he does, whether he is slave or free.
(Ephesians 6:5-8)

So do not throw away your confidence; it will be richly rewarded. You need to persevere so that when you have done the will of God, you will receive what he has promised. For in just a very little while, "He who is coming will come and will not delay. But my righteous one will live by faith. And if he shrinks back, I will not be pleased with him." But we are not of those who shrink back and are destroyed, but of those who believe and are saved.
(Hebrews 10:35-39)

The Apostle Paul writes, through the inspiration of the Holy Spirit:

I want to know Christ and the power of his resurrection and the fellowship of sharing in his sufferings, becoming like him in his death, and so, somehow, to attain to the resurrection from the dead.
(Philippians 3:10)

A Living Sacrifice: Chapter Ten

Paul knew that the only thing that mattered or counted in his life, or in life itself was knowing the LORD Jesus Christ and living in obedience to His will. Paul also acknowledges in Philippians chapter 3, as he concedes, that though he has not yet attained to all that the Lord will do, and that he has not yet been perfected, he presses on, that he might lay hold of that for which Christ Jesus has laid hold of him, and that he presses on toward the goal for the prize of the upward call of God, in Christ Jesus.

Paul goes on to say, ***therefore let us, as many as are mature, have this mind; and if in anything you think otherwise, God will reveal even this to you. Nevertheless, to the degree that we have already attained, let us walk by the same rule, let us be of the same mind.*** (Philippians 3:15-16)

Paul is speaking of a maturity that comes through discipleship and much commitment and devotion to the study, preaching and hearing of the Word of God in the power of the Holy Spirit, and thereby having the unity within the body of Christ that can only be ushered in and accomplished in the power of God. In conclusion, I write this, because it is the very reason the Holy Spirit has inspired me to write every chapter of this book. My hope is that we would understand that as Paul speaks of a maturity and of having the same mind, that this comes only through the understanding the Spirit imparts, and that as believers, we have been made spiritual and are now of the spirit, and no longer of the flesh. We cannot ignore the deeply spiritual things of God and how His power is made manifest in us by His Spirit, revealed to us through His Living Word.

Having said this, I believe in what the Scriptures reveal, and I agree with Paul, that it is the mature that understand, what it means to want to attain to the power of Christ's resurrection and the fellowship of His sufferings, being conformed to His death.

A Living sacrifice: Chapter Ten

It is the mature who understand, what it means to have been crucified with Christ, and can say, "***I no longer live but Christ lives in me, the life I live I live by faith in the Son of God, who loved me and gave Himself for me.***" It is the mature who can truly say, "*May I never boast except in the cross of our Lord Jesus Christ, through which the world has been crucified to me, and I to the world.*

It is the mature who understand, that we belong to Christ Jesus, bought and paid for by His precious blood, and that those who belong to Christ Jesus *have crucified the sinful nature with its passions and desires*, and that to live in Christ is to live by the Spirit, and we are those called to keep in step with the Spirit.

It is the mature, that understand that Christian *freedom* and *liberty* is for the glory of God, that having been released from the bondage of our very nature, and from the power of sin, we now have become a *new creation. A*nd having been born of the spirit, the Holy Spirit now empowers us to walk in obedience, leading us to surrender everything to God, that in this new found *freedom* and *liberty* we are called to live as bond servants of Christ, and slaves to His righteousness.

It is the mature who understand, that the living and active Word of God implores us, according to God's mercy, to lay down our bodies as living sacrifices, to understand the spiritual, that we are the righteousness of God, and that we are called to find out what pleases the Lord, and that now as a *new creation in* Christ, we are able to act upon the spiritual by the leading and control of His Spirit.

And finally, it is the mature that understand, that we are no longer to conform to the world, but we are to be transformed by the renewing of our minds, and in all of these things, it is to lead us to our very purpose here on earth, that we might test and approve the will of God, as we walk in Love, in Light, and in Wisdom, to accomplish His good, pleasing, and perfect will for His glory and for His glory alone.

A Living Sacrifice: Chapter Ten

Praise be to the God and Father of our Lord Jesus Christ, who has blessed us in the heavenly realms with every spiritual blessing in Christ. For he chose us in him before the creation of the world to be holy and blameless in his sight. In love he predestined us to be adopted as his sons through Jesus Christ, in accordance with his pleasure and will- to the praise of his glorious grace, which he has freely given us in the One he loves. In him we have redemption through his blood, the forgiveness of sins, in accordance with the riches of God's grace that he lavished on us with all wisdom and understanding. And he made known to us the mystery of his will according to his good pleasure, which he purposed in Christ, to be put into effect when the times will have reached their fulfillment-to bring all things in heaven and on earth together under one head, even Christ.
(Ephesians 1:3-10)

The Apostle Paul prays in the Spirit for the church, for each of us in the body of Christ:

For this reason I kneel before the Father, from whom every family in heaven and on earth derives its name. I pray that out of his glorious riches he may strengthen you with power through his Spirit in your inner being, so that Christ may dwell in your hearts through faith. And I pray that you, being rooted and established in love, may have power, together with all the Lord's holy people, to grasp how wide and long and high and deep is the love of Christ, and to know this love that surpasses knowledge--that you may be filled to the measure of all the fullness of God. Now to him who is able to do immeasurably more than all we ask or imagine, according to his power that is at work within us, to him be glory in the church and in Christ Jesus throughout all generations, for ever and ever! Amen.
(Ephesians 3:14-21)

A Living Sacrifice: Chapter Ten

I will leave you my friend, with these last three commandments of God, that you might have life, and life more abundant, according to His Spirit, His perfect will, and to His glory!

Walk in Love:

Therefore be imitators of God as dear children. And walk in love, as Christ also has loved us and given Himself for us, an offering and a sacrifice to God for a sweet-smelling aroma
(Ephesians 5:1-2)

Walk in Light:

For you were once darkness, but now you are light in the Lord. Walk as children of light (for the fruit of the Spirit is in all goodness, righteousness, and truth), finding out what is acceptable to the Lord. And have no fellowship with the unfruitful works of darkness, but rather expose them.
(Ephesians 5:8-11)

Walk in Wisdom:

See then that you walk circumspectly, not as fools but as wise, redeeming the time, because the days are evil. Therefore do not be unwise, but understand what the will of the Lord is. And do not be drunk with wine, in which is dissipation; but be filled with the Spirit, speaking to one another in psalms and hymns and spiritual songs, singing and making melody in your heart to the Lord, giving thanks always for all things to God the Father in the name of our Lord Jesus Christ, submitting to one another in the fear of God.
(Ephesians 5:15-21)

A Living Sacrifice: Chapter Ten

How do we impact this dark, lost, and dying world with the love of Christ? Will we walk according to the flesh, or will we now surrender all to Christ, that we might seek to be filled with the Holy Spirit, and walk not in the flesh, but in the Spirit's power? God has called us all to live a life of sacrifice. We are called to surrender all, that we might now be empowered, directed, guided, and under the influence of His Spirit. As we walk in the power of the Holy Spirit, we will be compelled to obedience no matter the cost, to do His will purposed for our lives, for His kingdom, and all to His glory!

> ***The Spirit of the LORD will rest on him-- the Spirit of wisdom and of understanding, the Spirit of counsel and of might, the Spirit of the knowledge and fear of the LORD—***
> ***(Isaiah 11:2)***

As "*A Conclusion of The Matter,*" I say farewell my friend, and may the grace and peace of our Lord and Savior Jesus Christ be with you. And by the power of His Spirit, (***that now rests upon you***), may you walk in **Love**, in **Light**, and in **Wisdom**, and may your life, your body, and your entire being, be ***A Living Sacrifice,*** holy and pleasing to God, for His glory! For this my friend, is your *spiritual act of worship.*

Made in the USA
Columbia, SC
22 October 2023